Megan Summers

COLECCIÓN *¡VIVA LA*

LIVE
SPANISH GRAMMAR
FOR
ENGLISH SPEAKERS

ELENA BÁRCENA
RONNA S. FEIT
TIMOTHY READ
BEATRIZ RODRÍGUEZ

en CLAVE | ELE

- **Directora Editorial:** Raquel Varela Méndez

Equipo Editorial

- **Edición:** Cándido Tejerina Martín
- **Diseño de interiores y maquetación:** Cantemar & Altegar
- **Consultoría lingüística y corrección de pruebas:** Amparo García Cocostegüe
- **Diseño de cubierta e ilustraciones:** DC Visual
- **Producción:** puertoNORTE-SUR, S.L.

Contents

FOREWORD

Welcome to the study of the Spanish language! You're about to learn to communicate effectively in Spanish while enjoying yourself. At least, that is our objective. Interested? Please, read on.

Objective, student profile and linguistic level

The goal of this book is to teach the foundations of the Spanish language, with particular attention to its grammar. The content is common to the majority of Spanish speaking communities in the world; regional varieties are avoided, except in one or two special cases that are labelled accordingly. Furthermore, unless otherwise stated, the book deals with standard Spanish, that is, the general language common to both oral and written communication in a neutral register, that is to say, neither too formal nor too colloquial. However, when the use of a given word, sequence, etc., has a particular connotation or is more suitable in a particular context, it is explicitly stated.

The book covers word formation, in the sense of how words take different endings to become plural, feminine, present, past, etc. It also describes the combinations of words needed to form correct phrases and sentences. It should be noted that Spanish is a rather regular language, which fortunately implies that a great deal of linguistic behaviour can be captured in elegant and cost-effective principles.

This book pretends to provide all the knowledge that a student needs to be able to undertake basic correct communication in Spanish as soon as possible. This is why every effort has been made to use words in a balanced way from the different areas of human activity, starting from the most widely used ones.

Therefore, for example, although the emphasis is placed on grammar, there are units on pronunciation and spelling, strategically interleaved with the rest, something which is crucial for the oral and written modalities respectively. There are also units on vocabulary and the language used in specific contexts and circumstances that are considered to be of particular interest. Attention is paid to the acquisition of new vocabulary, so while the most common words in the language (the equivalents of 'man', 'child', 'to go', etc.) appear in the examples and exercises more frequently than the rest, each exercise tends to include some new and useful vocabulary that must be looked up by the student in a bilingual dictionary and then learnt.

The book is particularly aimed at English native speakers. To start with, it is written in English, and Spanish examples are followed by their translation in English, especially in the early units of the book. Furthermore, the book has a contrastive approach, so for the majority of topics continuous reference is made to the equivalent principles and structures in English, pointing out the relevant similarities and differences as a device to assist the student in a conscious process of constructing new knowledge. However, in order to prevent an undesirable dependency on the student's mother tongue, he/she is warned in several units that it is not always possible to find one-to-one correspondences at a cross-linguistic level and that within each language there are many arbitrary aspects that cannot be translated literally into a target language; therefore, they have to be learnt by heart in the corresponding context.

No previous knowledge of Spanish is assumed on the part of the student, although the coverage and depth of the grammatical aspects of the language is such that it can be said that the level of the book starts at beginners' and finishes at (pre-)intermediate. Of course, it is easy to realise that this description of Spanish grammar is far from exhaustive. Rather, it is representative of the language. For each given topic there are several rules and exceptions that cannot be included in one single book. This book follows a broad and shallow approach (as opposed to narrow and deep), since it is preferable to have a rather general view of the most useful structures in the language that enable basic correct communication to be undertaken as soon as possible, rather than deepening too much and focusing on too little.

Every effort has been made to avoid unnecessary linguistic terminology. However, in order to help the reader understand certain terms, not only are they defined the first time they are used, but also a glossary has been included at the end of the book which contains simple explanations.

Structure of the book and of each unit

The book consists of fifty units or lessons, each one addressing a different linguistic topic. However, some topics are revisited further on in the book to present more advanced material that enables more complex or sophisticated expressions to be generated. Topics have been selected according to their relevance for communication, so that the student can start engaging in simple communicative acts as soon as possible. Following this criterion, the topics evolve from general to specific. The book is structured in blocks of approximately ten units, so that there is a parallel coverage of linguistic levels such as spelling and punctuation, vocabulary, word formation, sentence structure, functional language in communication, etc., to ensure that the student is always given a similar amount of detail of the different linguistic skills.

The organization of the topics also follows the logic that some of them need to have been assimilated in order to learn new ones, thus preventing the student from feeling unsure and possibly suffering in the future a 'structural collapse' of the linguistic knowledge structures that are currently being formed (as learning progresses).

Each unit is composed of two 'double pages'; the first (starting with the large unit title and an accompanying image) details the basic points related to the subject of the unit, and the second (with the smaller unit title) covers more advanced aspects of the subject in question. This mechanism enables the student to work with the book in two different ways: the first 'double page' of each unit can be studied first to provide a basic level of knowledge on a given topic and the second one studied immediately afterwards in order to achieve a deeper knowledge of the topic. Alternatively, the book can be studied in two 'rounds': one with the first set of 'double pages' and another one with the second

set. The exact approach adopted by the student will depend on his/her learning style and individual preferences.

Another methodological mechanism that has been included in the book is what is commonly known as the 'spiral approach' to language learning, that is to say, that as the student advances in the book, exercises involve structures that he/she has already learnt in previous units, hence testing and consolidating previously acquired linguistic knowledge. This strategy aims at preventing shallow learning by 'drill-and-practice', where the student may get the wrong idea about his/her own correct performance while doing the exercises due to over-monitorization, that is to say, that students perform more or less well while they are consciously practising a particular topic, but start making mistakes as soon as they have to apply the knowledge gained in an unknown situation. In order to avoid this problem, the exercises in this book are multi-task and accumulative in that they make the reader practise any topic that may have been covered up to that point in the book, along with the topic under study. The student who identifies an error related to a previously studied topic must go back to revise the corresponding unit.

All units are similar in length, the number of examples used, the type of exercises, etc. Progression is reflected in the decreasing use of English translations of new Spanish words. Such a reduction of supportive help as learning advances can be seen to follow what didactic specialists call 'scaffolding'. The structure of each unit reveals the complementary role of theory and practice in the book, where the emphasis is placed on the practice, giving importance to the communicative function of language. A given unit starts with very brief linguistic explanations of the corresponding topic, which are abundantly illustrated. The theoretical part is followed by a series of four exercises that a student must do before passing on to the next unit (or the second part of the current unit).

Study methodology

This book can be used as part of a standard classroom-based course or for self-study. It contains explicit and well illustrated explanations and the solutions to all the exercises in the book have been provided to allow for self correction. In order to encourage a student to actively participate in his/her own learning process and help control his/her progress, the student is asked to read the theory in each unit slowly and then do the corresponding exercises, checking the results against the answer key provided. Care should be taken to ensure that the student understands why mistakes have been made in the exercises to consolidate learning, before the next unit is started, for which it may be necessary to go back and re-read the theoretical explanation.

It should be noted that in order to allow for self correction, exercises are 'rather closed' (that is to say, the number of possible answers is highly restricted, something which is necessary due to the great flexibility in natural language production and the impossibility of anticipating every response that could be made). Since it is often the case that there is more than one possible answer, the preferred alternative is provided. The student should be aware, however, that occasionally another possible alternative answer may not have been contemplated. If in doubt, it is advisable that the theory of the given unit (or the corresponding one) is revised.

Since the coverage of this book is limited for practical reasons, its usefulness will be greatly expanded if the student has a bilingual dictionary to hand while working with it. It is recommended that, after looking up the endings of irregular verbs, the gender of new nouns, the meaning of the new words that appear in the exercises, etc., the results be noted in a personal notebook.

The combination of theory and practice facilitates the language learning process through the two well known approaches of conscious rule-based learning vs. practice-based acquisition. The goals of practice are, firstly, reinforcement: contributing to the understanding and assimilation of the linguistic topics; secondly, rehearsal: providing an opportunity for the student to apply what he has learnt as 'mock communication'; thirdly, controlling: good or bad performance can reveal the extent to which the unit has been successfully assimilated; fourthly and finally, learning: the exercises can deal with grammatical sub-cases not covered in the theoretical part.

Using exercises which differ substantially from the examples in the theoretical part enables the student to use his/her higher-order reasoning and associating and contrastive abilities, rather than merely his/her short term memory and capacity to repeat what is essentially the same sentence with minor changes. Furthermore, this type of practice expands the scope or coverage of the book, and hence its usefulness. In summary, it is advisable that the student views this book as a 'didactic reference' for Spanish, rather than an all-encompassing *vade mecum*.

Symbols

The following symbols are used in this book:

( ) ➡ optional elements and translations.

[] ➡ optional elements and translations within round brackets.

? ➡ dubious or stylistically inferior structures.

* ➡ ungrammatical structures.

/ ➡ alternatives and sounds.

Contact the authors

The authors will be pleased to receive constructive feedback on the book. You can contact us at the following address:

Dr. Elena Bárcena (coordinator)
Departamento de Filologías Extranjeras
y sus Lingüísticas, UNED
Senda del Rey 7
28040 Madrid, Spain

Acknowledgements

The authors would like to express their gratitude to Raquel Varela, Clara Andrade and Cándido Tejerina for their kindness and support throughout the preparation of this manuscript.

The authors

2004

1 YOUR AS AND BS
THE SPANISH ALPHABET

- The Spanish alphabet comprises twenty-nine letters:

LETTER	NAME	ENGLISH WORDS WITH APPROXIMATELY THIS SOUND		SPANISH WORDS
A, a	*a*	**A**nne		*a*vión
B, b	*be*	mo**b**ile		*b*e*b*é
C, c	*ce*	**c**ar, ba**th**ing	*c*asa	
Ch, ch	*che*	**ch**eese		*ch*ocolate
D, d	*de*	la**dd**er	*d*e*d*o	
E, e	*e*	**e**l**e**phant		*e*l*e*fant*e*
F, f	*efe*	co**ff**ee	*f*uente	
G, g	*ge*	ele**g**ant, **h**oney		*g*ato
H, h	*hache*	(mute)	*h*otel	
I, i	*i*	**E**ngland		*i*glesi*a*
J, j	*jota*	**h**ero	*j*abón	
K, k	*ka*	ma**k**er	*k*ilo	
L, l	*ele*	**l**ion	*l*eón	

LETTER	NAME	ENGLISH WORDS WITH APPROXIMATELY THIS SOUND		SPANISH WORDS
Ll, ll	*elle*	yard		*ll*uvia
M, m	*eme*	mother		*m*anzana
N, n	*ene*	banana		*n*aranja
Ñ, ñ	*eñe*	senior		ara*ñ*a
O, o	*o*	orchestra		*o*so
P, p	*pe*	supper		*p*ie
Q, q	*cu*	queue		*q*ueso
R, r; rr	*erre (doble)*	bar, curry		*r*osa
S, s	*ese*	Sunday		*s*ombrero
T, t	*te*	tomato		*t*omate
U, u	*u*	boot		*u*vas
V, v	*uve*	berry		*v*aca
W, w	*uve doble*	coward		ki*w*i
X, x	*equis*	exit		*x*ilófono
Y, y	*i griega*	mayor		*y*oyó
Z, z	*zeta*	Catherine		*z*apato

1 YOUR AS AND BS
THE SPANISH ALPHABET

- Since all nouns in Spanish are either masculine or feminine (see unit 7), you must know that letters are feminine, so their determiners and modifiers (e.g., articles, possessives, adjectives) must be feminine too.

  *Escribe un**a** "a" pequeñ**a*** (Write a small 'a').

- Several letters in the Spanish alphabet have different sounds depending on the vowel which comes after them.

  C can sound /k/ (before 'a', 'o' and 'u') or /z/ (before 'e' and 'i').

casa /k/ (house)	*cereza* /z/ (cherry)
coche /k/ (car)	*cisne* /z/ (swan)
cuchara /k/ (spoon)	

  G can sound /g/ (before 'a', 'o' and 'u') or /j/ (before 'e' and 'i').

gato /g/ (cat)	*gente* /j/ (people)
gota /g/ (drop)	*girafa* /j/ (giraffe)
gusano /g/ (worm)	

- There are several letters in the Spanish alphabet that are not found in the English one.

  Ch. It is identical to the combination of letters 'c+h' in English, in words like 'chance' and 'chewing gum'. It constitutes one letter in Spanish, although this difference does not have any relevance.

  chico (boy)
  chocolate (chocolate)
  ducha (shower)
  techo (roof)

  Ll. It is a double letter unrelated both to English 'l' in words like 'call' and 'wall', and to Spanish 'l' (e.g., *mala* is 'bad' in English and *malla*, 'mesh'). Its pronunciation is generally similar to that of English 'y'.

  llave (key)
  lluvia (rain)
  pollo (chicken)
  silla (chair)

Ñ. It is unrelated to both English and Spanish 'n' (e.g., *mono* is 'monkey' and *moño*, 'hair bun'). Its sound is rather similar to the sequence 'ni', 'ny' or 'nee' (as in 'canyon' or 'onion').

> *ñu* (gnu)
>
> *niña* (girl)
>
> *sueño* (dream)
>
> *piña* (pineapple)

RR. The presence of these two letters together can create a difference in meaning with respect to single 'r' (e.g., *caro* is 'expensive' and *carro*, 'cart'). Double 'r' always appears in the middle of the word; it is never the first or the last letter of the word.

> *perro* (dog)   *pero* (but)
>
> *perra* (bitch)   *pera* (pear)

Spanish 'r' can be pronounced weakly (similar to the English one but sharper) or strongly (a hard rolling sound, like the noise an engine makes). It is pronounced strongly at the beginning of a word and weak at the end. In the middle of a word, 'r' is pronounced strongly at the end of the syllable. At the beginning of the syllable, it depends on whether it is 'r' or 'rr': the former is weak and the latter, strong.

> *rosa* (rose) (strong)
>
> *carta* (letter) (strong)
>
> *comer* (to eat) (weak)
>
> *caro* (expensive) (weak)

H. It requires special attention because it is completely mute in Spanish, so two words with the same letters except for an 'h' have identical pronunciation. 'H' is common between vowels; however, it can only be predicted in words starting with sequences like *helio-*, *hetero-*, *hipo-* and *hiper-*.

> *hasta* (until)   *asta* (flagpole)
>
> *hola* (hello)   *ola* (wave)
>
> *haya* (beech tree)   *aya* (governess)
>
> *ahora* (now)   *hipermercado* (hypermarket)

W. Conversely, 'w' is a very uncommon letter in Spanish, only used in the initial position of a few words of clear Angloamerican origin. Some of them refer to popular trademarks.

> *walkie-talkie* (walkie-talkie)   *waterpolo* (water polo)

THE CAT SAT ON THE MAT
THE SPANISH SENTENCE

- The Spanish sentence is similar to the English one, although the order of the words is far more flexible.

  It generally consists of a subject (the 'agent' or 'doer' of an action) followed by a verb plus information about where, when, how, etc. that action took place.

SUBJECT	VERB	COMPLEMENTS
Juan	*ama*	*a María.*

- The verb (e.g., 'to buy') is typically followed by the 'direct object' of the action (the object, person, etc. directly related to it, e.g., 'a present'), then the 'indirect object' of the action (its 'recipient', e.g., 'for her mother'), and finally the adverbials, which provide contextual information about the instrument, the location, the time, etc. (e.g. 'at the shop').

  María + compra + un regalo + para su madre + en la tienda.

  Mary + buys   + a present + for her mother + at the shop.

1. Fill in the sentences with the correct word or words from the box.

> Papá (Daddy) – al fútbol – escribe (writes) – El niño (The boy) – abre (opens)

1. María **abre** el paraguas (the umbrella).
2. _Papá_ ✓ compra el periódico (buys the newspaper).
3. Mi hermano juega (My brother plays) _al fútbol_ . ✓
4. _El niño_ ✓ monta a caballo (rides a horse).
5. Su mujer (His wife) _escribe_ ✓ novelas de terror (thriller novels).

2. Reorder the pieces of information to make correct sentences.

1. el autobús (the bus) / espero (wait for) / yo (I) ➡ **Yo espero el autobús.**
2. por el campo (in the fields) / camina (walks) / Marta
   Marta camina por el campo. ✓
3. paella / comen (eat) / Susana y Carlos
   Susana y Carlos comen paella. ✓
4. a bailar (dancing) / van (go) / los amigos (the friends)
   Los amigos van a bailar. ✓
5. cerca de aquí (near here) / vive (lives) / mi madre (my mother)
   Mi madre vive cerca de aquí. ✓

3. Correct the order of the elements in the following sentences.

1. a Margarita / ama (loves) / Julián. ➡ **Julián ama a Margarita.**
2. Antonio y Juan / en el restaurante (at the restaurant) / comen (eat)
   Antonio y Juan comen en el restaurante. ✓
3. corto (cut) / el pastel (the cake) / yo (I)
   Yo corto el pastel. ✓
4. canciones románticas (romantic songs) / Ricardo / canta (sings)
   Ricardo canta canciones románticas. ✓
5. estudia (studies) / Laura / en la biblioteca (at the library)
   Laura estudia en la biblioteca. ✓

4. Match the two columns to form a sentence.

1. Ana habla (Anne speaks)   a) 30 años (30 years old). ✓
2. Yo tengo (I am)   b) Laura. ✓
3. Hola, soy (Hi, I am)   c) español (Spanish). ✓
4. José trabaja (Joseph works)   d) regalos (presents). ✓
5. Mis amigos compran (My friends buy)   e) en IBM (at IBM). ✓

2 THE CAT SAT ON THE MAT
THE SPANISH SENTENCE

- Spanish sentences are flexible and almost every order is acceptable. It often depends on which information is important to the speaker, which tends to appear first.

    Los martes + yo + voy + al cine + con mis amigos.

    (On Tuesdays I go to the cinema with my friends.)

    Yo + voy al cine + los martes + con mis amigos.

    Yo + voy al cine + con mis amigos + los martes.

- Complements may be introduced by different prepositions (***a*** [to], ***en*** [in], ***de*** [of], etc.). The direct object is also introduced by ***a*** with most verbs when it refers to an animate definite entity (people, high-order animals, etc.). The indirect object may be introduced by ***a*** or ***para***.

    *Yo compro flores **para** mi novia* (I buy flowers for my girlfriend).

    Yo veo la television (I watch television).

    *Yo veo **a** mi sobrina* (I see my niece).

    Yo necesito una silla (I need a chair).

    *Yo necesito **a** María* (I need María).

    Yo contesto la encuesta (I answer the survey).

    *Yo contesto **a** Daniel* (I answer Daniel).

- When ***a*** and ***de*** are followed by the article ***el*** (see unit 6), they are joined together in one word: ***al*** and ***del***, respectively.

    *Yo espero **al** niño* (I wait for the boy).

    *Yo espero **a la** niña* (I wait for the girl).

    *Él viene **del** cine* (He comes from the cinema).

    *Él viene **de la** ópera* (He comes from the opera).

5. Put the preposition *a* in the sentences below if necessary.

1. Veo (I see) **a** Elena.
2. Amo (I love) __a__ la naturaleza (nature).
3. Amo (I love) __a__ mi familia (my family).
4. Hablo (I speak) _____ italiano (Italian).
5. Hablo (I speak to) _____ mi padre (my father).

6. Correct the following sentences if necessary.

1. Escucho mi prima (I listen to my cousin). ➡ *Escucho a mi prima.*
2. Doy de comer el bebé con una cuchara (I feed the baby with a spoon).

   Doy de comer al el bebé con una cuchara.
3. Leo el periódico con gafas (I read the newspaper with glasses).

   _____
4. Pinto a un cuadro abstracto (I paint an abstract painting).

   _____
5. Duermo la siesta (I take a nap).

   _____

7. Put *a, al, de* or *del* in the following sentences, making whatever corrections are necessary.

1. Vamos (Let's go) **al** teatro esta noche (theatre tonight).
2. Veo (I see) __a__ mi amiga Isabel (my friend Elizabeth).
3. Vengo (I come) __de__ la peluquería (the hairdresser's).
4. Vosotros volvéis (You come back) __del__ trabajo (work).
5. Juegan (They play) con los hijos __del__ vecino (neighbour).

8. Reorder the pieces of information in the most logical order.

1. en el circo / los payasos / trabajan ➡ *Los payasos trabajan en el circo.*
2. compra / mi madre / en la tienda / una corbata

   mi madre compra una corbata en la tienda.
3. a las fiestas/ Beatriz y Cristina / del pueblo / van

   Beatriz y Cristiana van a las fiestas del pueblo.
4. mis amigos / la televisión / ven / en el salón

   mis amigos ven la televisión en el salón.
5. en la consulta / el doctor / a los pacientes / atiende

   el doctor atiende a los pacientes en la consulta.

3   I LEARN, YOU TEACH
SPANISH VERBS. THE PRESENT TENSE

- Spanish verbs in their infinitive form are not preceded by a particle like in English ('to eat', 'to write'…); they finish with the letters **-ar**, **-er** or **-ir**. These three categories are called 'conjugations'. Therefore, all verbs belong either to the first (**-ar**), second (**-er**) or third (**-ir**) conjugation according to their ending.

-AR	-ER	-IR
amar (to love)	*comprender* (to understand)	*abrir* (to open)
estudiar (to study)	*beber* (to drink)	*vivir* (to live)
cantar (to sing)	*comer* (to eat)	*batir* (to beat)

- The endings of verbal forms in Spanish sentences vary greatly according to factors such as the time (if it is present, past, etc.), but also to the subject (if it is me, you, him, etc.) and the conjugation (if it is the first, the second or the third one). Let us see the endings that replace the infinitive ones for the simple present in each conjugation.

  I love ➡ *Yo am**o***   We love ➡ *Nosotros am**amos***
  You love ➡ *Tú am**as***   You love ➡ *Vosotros am**áis***
  He loves ➡ *Él am**a***   They love ➡ *Ellos am**an***

  I drink ➡ *Yo beb**o***   We drink ➡ *Nosotros beb**emos***
  You drink ➡ *Tú beb**es***   You drink ➡ *Vosotros beb**éis***
  He drinks ➡ *Él beb**e***   They drink ➡ *Ellos beb**en***

  I live ➡ *Yo viv**o***   We live ➡ *Nosotros viv**imos***
  You live ➡ *Tú viv**es***   You live ➡ *Vosotros viv**ís***
  He lives ➡ *Él viv**e***   They live ➡ *Ellos viv**en***

1. Conjugate the following verbs:

	Yo	Tú	Él	Nosotros	Vosotros	Ellos
1. pasear (to walk)	paseo	paseas	pasea	paseamos	paseáis	pasean ✓
2. subir (to go up)	subo	subes	sube	subimos	subís	suben ✓
3. correr (to run)	corro	corres	corre	corremos	corréis	corren ✓
4. partir (to leave)	parto	partes	parte	partimos	partís	parten ✓
5. hablar (to speak)	hablo	hablas	habla	hablamos	habláis	hablan ✓

2. Fill the slots with a suitable personal pronoun.

1. *Nosotros/nosotras* esperamos la respuesta.
2. _Ellos/Ellas_ compran comida.
3. _Vosotros\Vosotras_ jugáis al fútbol.
4. _él\Ella_ comprende el ejercicio.
5. _Tú_ vendes coches.

3. Match the following chunks to make grammatical and meaningful sentences.

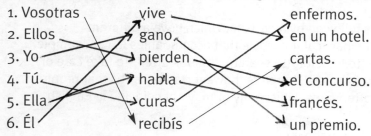

1. Vosotras   vive   enfermos.
2. Ellos   gano   en un hotel.
3. Yo   pierden   cartas.
4. Tú   habla   el concurso.
5. Ella   curas   francés.
6. Él   recibís   un premio.

4. Write the correct form of the verb in brackets.

1. Yolanda no **vive** (vivir) en Madrid (Yolanda doesn't live in Madrid).
2. Nosotros ___paseamos___ (pasear) por el campo en primavera (We walk round the countryside in spring).
3. Mis primos ___deben___ (deber) ir al dentista (My cousins must go to the dentist).
4. Yo ___como___ (comer) tortilla de patatas (I eat Spanish omelette).
5. Vosotros ___preparáis___ (preparar) el equipaje para las vacaciones (You pack up for the holidays).

17

I LEARN, YOU TEACH
SPANISH VERBS. THE PRESENT TENSE

- All the verbs in the simple present that belong to a given conjugation take the same endings; for example, *yo beso, tú besas, yo como, tú comes, yo decido, tú decides,* etc.

- If a verb does not follow all the endings for its conjugation, it is called an 'irregular verb'. There are not many irregular verbs in Spanish but they are the most common ones (the equivalents of 'to do', 'to go', 'to have', etc. ➠ *hacer, ir, tener,* etc.) and must be learnt separately.

  I do / I make ➠ *Yo hago*   We do / We make ➠ *Nosotros hacemos*
  You do / I make ➠ *Tú haces*   You do / You make ➠ *Vosotros hacéis*
  He does / I makes ➠ *Él hace*   They do / They make ➠ *Ellos hacen*

  I have ➠ *Yo tengo*   We have ➠ *Nosotros tenemos*
  You have ➠ *Tú tienes*   You have ➠ *Vosotros tenéis*
  He has ➠ *Él tiene*   They have ➠ *Ellos tienen*

- The degree of irregularity of a verb varies greatly; sometimes there are only a few differences with respect to the standard conjugation (see the annexe of irregular verbs).

- In English there are verbs followed by a particle, which have a different meaning depending on the particular particle that accompanies it. For example, 'to look' is different from 'to look for' (to search), 'to look after' (to take care of), etc. This does not exist in Spanish. There are, however, some verbs that require a particular preposition afterwards, which may or may not coincide in English, and vice versa:

  Cuento con vosotros (I count on you).

  Me alegro de verte (I am glad to see you).

  Vosotras confiáis en Miguel (You trust Michael).

  Nosotros desconfiamos de Alberto (We mistrust Albert).

  Esperas una oportunidad (You wait for an opportunity).

- It should be emphasized that prepositions are arbitrary words with little or no meaning, and may or not appear in the equivalent sentence in another language. Also, note that two related verbs may require different prepositions (like the equivalents of 'trust' and 'mistrust' above). Therefore, it is important to learn new verbs together with the preposition they take.

5. Mark the following verbal forms as regular (R) or irregular (I).

1. Amas (love) ➞ R
2. Mueven (move) ➞ ____
3. Vivo (live) ➞ R
4. Perdemos (lose) ➞ ____
5. Vengo (come) ➞ ____

6. Bebemos (drink) ➞ R
7. Ríen (laugh) ➞ ____
8. Sientes (feel) ➞ ____
9. Plancha (iron) ➞ ____
10. Pensáis (think) ➞ ____

6. Correct the following sentences if necessary (the infinitive is given to help you).

1. Ellas escuchen (escuchar) la música (They listen to music). *Ellas escuchan la música.*
2. Tú hagas (hacer) pasteles (You make cakes). Tú haces pasteles.
3. Nosotros cocinemos (cocinar) pescado (We cook fish). Nosotros cocinamos pescado.
4. Vosotras bailamos (bailar) flamenco (You dance flamenco). Vosotras bailáis flamenco.
5. Yo nadamos (nadar) en el mar (I swim in the sea). Yo nado en el mar.

7. Decide which preposition is correct.

1. No te rías (de)/con mí. (Don't laugh at me).
2. Confío con/(en) mis amigos (I trust my friends).
3. Julia se casó a/(con) Jorge ayer (Julia married George yesterday).
4. Me alegro con/(de) verte tan bien de salud. (I'm glad to see you so healthy).
5. Estamos hablando (de)/en nuestros problemas (We're talking about our problems).

8. Add a suitable preposition if necessary.

1. Sueño (I dream) *con* Brad Pitt.
2. Me entristece (I am sad) _____ tu fracaso (for your failure).
3. El pastel contiene (The cake has) _____ dos tipos de fruta (two types of fruit).
4. El premio consiste (The prize consists of) _____ un viaje alrededor del mundo (a trip around the world).
5. Dependen (They depend on) _____ sus padres (their parents).

19

4 SUBJECTS OF H. M. THE SENTENCE
SUBJECT PERSONAL PRONOUNS

- As seen in the previous unit, in Spanish, Like in English, there are six 'grammatical persons': the speaker, the addressee and somebody that is neither of them, all of which can be one or more than one.

- Entities can be fully expressed (e.g., 'Majorca', 'the dogs', etc.) or alluded to via personal pronouns. The personal pronouns that can be the subject of a sentence are the following:

1st person singular	*Yo* (I)
2nd person singular	*Tú* (You, informal) / *Usted* (You, formal)
3rd person singular	*Él* (He)
3rd person singular	*Ella* (She)
1st person plural	*Nosotros/Nosotras* (We)
2nd person plural	*Vosotros/Nosotras* (You, informal) / *Ustedes* (You, formal)
3rd person plural	*Ellos/Ellas* (They)

escribir   *escriber*

1. Fill each gap below with a suitable personal pronoun.

1. **El/ella** comenta el problema (... comments on the problem).
2. **Ellos\Ellas** trabajan de modelos (... work as models).
3. **El\Ella** lleva pantalones (... wears trousers).
4. _____ compras pulseras (... buy bracelets).
5. **Yo** cambio dinero (... exchange money).

2. Substitute the subject by a personal pronoun in the following sentences.

1. Raquel crece rápido. ➡ **Ella** crece rápido. (Rachel is growing quickly.)
2. Susana y Francisco suben una montaña. ➡ **Ellos** suben una montaña.
   (Susan and Francis are climbing a mountain.)
3. Mi amiga y yo cantamos ópera. ➡ **Nosotros** cantamos ópera. (My friend
   and I sing opera.)
4. Marta y tú voláis con Air Europa. ➡ **Nosotros** voláis con Air Europa.
   (Marta and you are flying with Air Europa.)
5. Roberto chupa un caramelo. ➡ **Él** chupa un caramelo. (Robert is
   sucking on a sweet.)

3. Put the following sentences in the plural (e.g., 1st person singular ➡ 1st person plural, etc.).

1. Yo veo la pizarra. ➡ **Nosotros vemos la pizarra.** (I see the blackboard.)
2. Tú saludas a alguien. ➡ **Vosotros saludas a alguien.** (You are greeting somebody.)
3. Él abre la puerta. ➡ **Ellos abre la puerta.** (He is opening the door.)
4. Ella lava el coche. ➡ **Ellas lava el coche.** (She is washing the car.)
5. Usted es muy importante. ➡ **Ustedes es muy importante.** (You are very important.)

4. Correct any incorrect statement changing the verb form if necessary.

1. Yo juegas con un muñeco (I / play with a puppet). **Yo juego con un muñeco.**
2. Ellos vemos la televisión (They / watch TV). **Ellos ven la televisión.**
3. Tú bailas salsa (You / dance salsa). **Tú bailan salsa.**
4. Ella escribo una carta (She / write a letter). **Ella escribe una carta.**
5. Vosotras bebéis agua (You / drink water). **Vosotros bebéis agua.**

4   SUBJECTS OF H. M. THE SENTENCE
SUBJECT PERSONAL PRONOUNS

- As mentioned in unit 1, all Spanish nouns belong to the masculine or feminine gender, even those corresponding to objects.

MASCULINE NOUNS	FEMININE NOUNS
hombre (man)	*mujer* (woman)
camarero (waiter)	*camarera* (waitress)
gato (he-cat)	*gata* (she-cat)
pico (peak)	*cola* (tail)
puerto (port)	*playa* (beach)

- As a general rule, the subject personal pronoun is eliminated. This is possible because Spanish verbal endings distinguish the grammatical person.

  (Yo) Hoy cumplo 23 años (Today I am 23 years old).

  Carmen está aquí. (Ella) Acaba de llegar (Carmen is here. She has just arrived).

  (Nosotros) Comemos una manzana (We eat an apple).

- In fact, the pronoun is only used for emphasis or to help the listener interpret what is being said in an ambiguous situation.

  Compra una moto (She or he buys a motorbike).

  Ella *compra la moto* (She buys the motorbike).

  Nosotras *damos los regalos* (We women give the presents – implying: not anybody else).

- The gender is explicitly expressed in the three plural persons: pronouns ending in **-os** are masculine and those ending in **-as** are feminine. Therefore, for example, if you are talking to a group of ladies, you would address them as *vosotras*. However, if there is a group of people and at least one of them is male, the masculine pronoun is used.

  *Nosot****ros*** *comemos una manzana* (We eat an apple).

  *Vosot****ras*** *estudiáis* (You [girls] study).

- There are two ways to refer to your listener depending on the relationship you have with him/her. If it is a formal one, because you do not know him/her well, he/she is elderly, or your superior at work, you address him/her as *usted* as a sign of respect. If, on the contrary, he/she is a youngster or somebody the same age, a relative, a friend, or a colleague from work, you address him/her as *tú*. It is common to see the abbreviations *Ud.* or *Vd.* for *usted* in writing. They are read *'usted'* (see unit 20 for the Latin American equivalents).

  Estás invitado a la fiesta (You [colloquial] are invited to the party).

  Vd. *está invitado a la inauguración* (You [formal] are invited to the opening ceremony).

  Está invitado a la inauguración (You [formal] are / he/she is invited to the opening ceremony).

5. Choose the correct personal pronoun according to the gender.

1. Catalina y Carmen están tristes. Nadie habla con ~~ellos~~/ellas. (Katherine and Carmen are sad. Nobody talks to them.)

2. Mi perro está enfermo. Tengo que ir con ~~ella~~/él al veterinario. (My dog is sick. I have to take it to the vet.)

3. La tía de Pablo está en la cafetería y Juan está con ~~ello~~/ella. (Paul's aunt is in the café and John is with her.)

4. ¿Tienes muchos problemas? No pienses en ellos/~~ellas~~ ahora. (Do you have a lot of problems? Don't think about them now.)

5. Esta mesa está sucia. No pongas nada encima de él/~~ella~~. (This table is dirty. Don't put anything on top of it.)

6. Indicate the gender of the following nouns and translate them into English. Then make up a sentence by conjugating the verb in brackets.

1. caballo MASCULINE — horse ⟹ El caballo descansa. (descansar)

2. camión _Masculine - lorry_ ⟹ ~~Este~~ La camión parado _____ (parar)

3. cama _Feminine - bed_ ⟹ _____ cama se _romp_ _____ (romper)

4. camino _Masculine - path_ ⟹ _____ camino _____ (acabar)

5. calle _Masculine - street_ ⟹ _____ calle _____ (empezar)

7. Put the verb in the 2nd person correct form according to the data provided.

1. Usted fríe (freír; singular formal) los huevos para todos (... are frying eggs for everybody).

2. _____ (descansar; plural formal) en una cama (... rest in a bed).

3. _____ (sonreír; singular informal) delante del espejo (... smile in front of the mirror).

4. _____ (diseñar; plural informal) vestidos para niñas (... design dresses for girls).

5. _____ (limpiar; plural formal) las alfombras con la aspiradora (... vacuum the carpets).

8. Choose the correct form: *tú, usted, ustedes.*

1. Tú eres como mi hermana (You are like my sister).

2. _Usted_ es un empleado muy trabajador (You are a hard working employee).

3. _tú_ tienen que llegar puntuales (You have to arrive on time).

4. _tú_ comes mucha pasta (You eat a lot of pasta).

5. _usted_ merece un castigo (You deserve to be punished).

5

3, 2, 1... 0!
CARDINAL NUMBERS

CINCO, CUATRO...

- The following table shows the numbers in Spanish:

0 cero	10 diez	20 veinte	30 treinta
1 uno	11 once	21 veintiuno	31 treinta y uno
2 dos	12 doce	22 veintidós	32 treinta y dos
3 tres	13 trece	23 veintitrés	33 treinta y tres
4 cuatro	14 catorce	24 veinticuatro	34 treinta y cuatro
5 cinco	15 quince	25 veinticinco	35 treinta y cinco
6 seis	16 dieciséis	26 veintiséis	36 treinta y seis
7 siete	17 diecisiete	27 veintisiete	37 treinta y siete
8 ocho	18 dieciocho	28 veintiocho	38 treinta y ocho
9 nueve	19 diecinueve	29 veintinueve	39 treinta y nueve

- The rest of the numbers up to 100 follow the same pattern as 30+ above. Note that counting by hundreds does not go beyond 999 in Spanish. It is not possible to say, for example, the equivalent of 'twelve hundred' for 1200.

40 cuarenta	100 cien	500 quinientos
41 cuarenta y uno	101 ciento uno	600 seiscientos
50 cincuenta	102 ciento dos	700 setecientos
60 sesenta	199 ciento noventa y nueve	800 ochocientos
70 setenta	200 doscientos	900 novecientos
80 ochenta	201 doscientos uno	1.000 mil
90 noventa	300 trescientos	1.001 mil uno
99 noventa y nueve	400 cuatrocientos	1.100 mil cien

- Note that **y** (and) appears between the tens and the units.

1. Relate the number to the corresponding written form.

a) 256
b) 844
c) 19
d) 390
e) 947

diecinueve.
trescientos noventa.
novecientos cuarenta y siete.
doscientos cincuenta y seis.
ochocientos cuarenta y cuatro.

2. Write all the numbers between 60 and 70.

60 – sesenta

sesenta y uno

sesenta y dos

sesenta y tres

sesenta y cuatro

sesenta y cinco

sesenta y seis

sesenta y siete

sesenta y ocho

sesenta y nueve

setenta

3. Write the numerical Spanish equivalents of the following figures.

a) Cincuenta y tres ➟ 53
b) Setecientos veinticuatro ➟ 724
c) Dieciocho ➟ 18
d) Novecientos trece ➟ 913
e) Mil tres ➟ 3000

4. Translate the following numbers.

a) Seventy-five ➟ Setenta y cinco.
b) Thirty-one ➟ treinta y uno
c) A hundred and twelve ➟ cien doce
d) Two hundred and one ➟ doscientoas uno
e) One thousand two hundred and thirty-three ➟ mil doscientos y trienta y tres.

5 3, 2, 1... 0!
CARDINAL NUMBERS

- Let us see the pattern for the numbers above one thousand.

2.000 dos mil	100.000 cien mil
2.001 dos mil uno	1.000.000 un millón
9.000 nueve mil	100.000.000 cien millones
10.000 diez mil	1.000.000.000 mil millones
11.000 once mil	1.000.000.000.000 un billón

- Unlike English, in Spanish a comma introduces decimals and a dot separates thousands.

  100.000 (a hundred thousand).

  100,00 (one hundred).

  3.502 (three thousand five hundred and two).

  3,502 (three point five hundred and two).

  123.456,789 (one hundred and twenty three thousand four hundred and fifty six point seven eight nine: *ciento veintitrés mil cuatrocientos cincuenta y seis con setecientos ochenta y nueve*).

- Note that decimals in Spanish are introduced by the preposition **con** (point) and tend to be referred to number by number when there are many.

- The form of numbers is invariable in the sentence with a few exceptions:
  – Firstly, numbers ending in *-uno* and *-cientos* take the same gender as the noun they refer to: *-una* and *-cientas*.

    Cuarenta y una fotografías (41 photos).

    Doscientas cuarenta y siete cosas (247 things).

  – Secondly, when followed by a masculine noun, '*-uno*' turns into '*-ún*'.

    Quiero cuarenta y uno (I want 41).

    Tienes veintiún invitados (You have 21 guests).

  – Thirdly, *millón* and *billón* are nouns, so they take *millones* and *billones* as plurals. They link to another noun through the preposition **de**. It is also possible to say *cientos* (hundreds), and *miles* (thousands) if they are not preceded or followed by any other number.

    Doscientos millones de personas (two hundred million people).

    Tengo miles (I have thousands).

    Mil billones de sonrisas (a thousand billion smiles).

    Tengo cien mil (I have a hundred thousand).

5. Write the full word equivalents of the following Spanish figures.

a) 457 ➡ *cuatrocientos cincuenta y siete.*

b) 2.307 ➡ <u>dos mil trescientos y siete</u>

c) 257.988 ➡ <u>doscientos cincunta siete mil novecientos ochenta y ocho.</u>

d) 500.002 ➡ <u>cincocientos mil y dos.</u>

e) 987.654 ➡ <u>novecientos ochenta siete mil siescientos cincunta y cuatro.</u>

6. Correct any of the following quantities if necessary.

a) Cuatrocientasymil quinientas veintisiete. ➡ **Cuatrocientas mil quinientas veintisiete.**

b) Mil novecientos treintaicinco.

<u>Mil novecientos treinta y cinco.</u>

c) Dos millones seiscientosmil ochocientos veinticuatro.

<u>Doscientos millones seiscientos mil ochocientos veinticuatro.</u> (dos mil)

d) Novecientos noventa y siete.

<u>Novecientos noventa y siete.</u>

e) Sesentaiun millones trescientas veinticincomil novecientas quince.

<u>sesesentos millones trescientas veinticinco mil novecientas quince.</u> (siete mil)

7. Write the numerical equivalents of the following quantities paying attention to the Spanish punctuation.

a) Trece mil millones novecientos catorce con setecientos dos. ➡ **13.000.000.914,702**

b) Nueve mil quinientos veinticuatro con catorce. ➡ <u>9</u>

c) Un billón novecientos millones cuatrocientos catorce mil con cuatro. ➡
<u>1.900.000.000.414,4</u>

d) Cinco con noventa y tres. ➡ <u>5,93</u>

e) Trescientos mil treinta y tres con trece. ➡ <u>300.033,13</u>

8. Write the full word equivalents of the following numbers paying attention to the Spanish punctuation.

a) 964.762.400,1 ➡ <u>nueve mil millones setecientos sesenta y dos</u> (sesenta y cuatro)

b) 374.500.000,43 ➡ _____

c) 23.598.000.433,122 ➡ _____

d) 900.000.000,01 ➡ _____

e) 64.834,938 ➡ _____

6 LA, LA, LA, LAAAAA...
INDEFINITE AND DEFINITE ARTICLES

LA LUNA Y UNAS ESTRELLAS.

- Nouns are often preceded by articles, like in the sentence 'I don't want *a* jewel, I want *the* jewel in the shop window', which implies that it is not any indefinite jewel I fancy, but a particular, definite one I have already seen somewhere. The Spanish articles are the following:

	INDEFINITE		DEFINITE	
	SINGULAR	**PLURAL**	**SINGULAR**	**PLURAL**
MASCULINE	un	unos	el	los
FEMININE	una	unas	la	las

*Alquilo **un** camión* (I hire a lorry).

*Cojo **el** autobús* (I catch the bus).

*Necesitan **una** silla* (They need a chair).

*Pone **la** mesa* (He/she sets the table).

Quiero voluntarios (I need volunteers).

***Los** vecinos son amables* (The neighbours are kind).

*Hablo a **unas** señoras* (I speak to some ladies).

***Las** novias asienten* (The girlfriends nod).

- Since the plural indefinite articles add no information, they are frequently omitted, in which case the reference is particularly vague.

  *Necesito **unos** vasos* (I need some glasses – probably not too many).

  Necesito vasos (I need glasses – it could be two or two million).

- As mentioned in unit 4, masculine is the default gender in Spanish so if there is a group of people (or animals) and at least one of them is male, the masculine article is used.

1. Put the corresponding definite and indefinite article in front of each noun below.

1. *La* / *Una* playa
2. _____ / _____ nube
3. _____ / _____ primas
4. _____ / _____ ruedas
5. _____ / _____ juguete

2. Correct the following sentences if necessary.

1. Cierro las puerta. _____
2. Buscamos la casa en Madrid para vivir (to live in).

   _____

3. Unos pájaros vuelan con (with) las alas, no con un pico.

   _____

4. Necesitas la novia nueva. _____
5. No entiendo la frase, repítela (repeat it).

   _____

3. Add a suitable article if necessary.

1. Tengo que comprar vasos.   _____
2. Niña es muy alta.   _____
3. Viven en casa muy bonita.   _____
4. Animales del zoo tienen hambre.   _____
5. Juan conduce coche azul.   _____

4. Make grammatical sentences out of the following chunks.

1. Nosotras / mirar / paisaje. ➡ *Nosotras miramos el paisaje.*

   _____

2. Ellos / estudiar / idiomas.

   _____

3. Mujer / mirar / reloj.

   _____

4. Pedro y Guillermo / abrir / negocio.

   _____

5. Tú / comer / bocadillo.

   _____

6

LA, LA, LA, LAAAAA...
INDEFINITE AND DEFINITE ARTICLES

- The definite article can be used to refer generically to all the entities of a given kind, even before an adjective. The plural can also be used in a collective sense.

    El león es mi animal favorito (The lion is my favourite animal).

    Los leones rugen fuerte (Lions roar loudly).

    El vino tiene alcohol (Wine has alcohol).

    Los vinos de España son excelentes (Spanish wines are excellent).

    El poderoso no tiene necesariamente razón (The powerful are not necessarily right).

    Los inteligentes suelen ser buenos (The intelligent are usually good).

- Other general uses of the definite article which differ from English include the following:

    – Abstract nouns: *Odio **la** violencia* (I hate violence).

    – Weekdays: *Descansas **los** domingos* (You rest on Sundays).

    – Parts of the body: *Abre **la** boca* (He opens his mouth).

    – A qualified proper noun: ***El** pobre Daniel llora* (Poor Daniel cries).

- The indefinite article is used for qualified abstract nouns and approximate numbers, and omitted when expressing origin, rank and occupation.

    *Siento **un** amor apasionado* (I feel passionate love).

    *Tenemos **unos** cien sellos* (We have around a hundred stamps).

    Pareces alemán (You look German).

    Soy médico (I am a doctor).

    Es teniente (He is a lieutenant).

- Feminine nouns starting with accented or stressed 'a-' or 'ha'- take *el* and *un* instead of *la* and *una* if they occur immediately before. The accented syllable is highlighted in the words below.

un **al**ma (a soul)	las **al**mas (the souls)
esta **al**ma (this soul)	la blanca **al**ma (the white soul)
el **ha**cha (the axe)	unas **ha**chas (some axes)
esta **ha**cha (this axe)	la pequeña **ha**cha (the little axe)
la ha**ri**na (the flour)	la amabi**li**dad (kindness)
una a**lon**dra (the lark)	una ha**ma**ca (the hammock)

5. Fill in the gaps with a suitable article if necessary.

1. _La_ carne sabe deliciosa.

2. Parecemos _____ portugueses.

3. Necesitas _____ sillas aquí.

4. Estudia _____ jueves.

5. _____ música relaja a _____ personas.

6. Translate the following sentences paying attention to the article that is most suitable.

1. She calls the firemen. ⟹ _(Ella) llama a los bomberos._

2. Friends always help. _____

3. Raise your arm. _____

4. Sweet Juliet recites poems. _____

5. Fish are dumb. _____

7. Make whatever corrections are necessary in the following sentences.

1. El toro tiene la asta rota. _____

2. Tengo una hambre voraz. _____

3. Bebe un gran vaso de agua. _____

4. El harina es blanca. _____

5. El altura del edificio es excesiva. _____

8. Make grammatical sentences out of the following chunks.

1. Altos / jugar / baloncesto. _____

2. María / conducir / coche nuevo. _____

3. Manuel / trabajar / fines de semana. _____

4. Leñador / tener / hacha. _____

5. Frida / ser/ alemana. _____

7 IS IT A BOY OR A GIRL?

THE GENDER OF NOUNS

- As mentioned in units 1 and 4, all nouns in Spanish are masculine or feminine, singular or plural. These features have important consequences because most modifiers of a given noun change according to the gender and number of the noun. Only a few of them are invariable, e.g., *estándar* (standard) (used with masculine and feminine, singular and plural nouns, although *estándares* also exists) and *gris* (gray) (used with masculine and feminine nouns; the form *grises* is used for both plurals).

- The gender is easy to guess in the case of sexed entities: people or high-order animals. The masculine and feminine counterparts of a given noun may be identical, completely different words, or only differ in the ending. In the last case, just as verbs are looked up in the dictionary by the infinitive form, nouns in dictionaries are masculine (and singular) by default.

MASCULINE	FEMININE
profesor (male teacher)	*profesora* (female teacher)
abuelo (grandfather)	*abuela* (grandmother)
monje (monk)	*monja* (nun)
toro (bull)	*vaca* (cow)

- As we descend into less familiar animals, objects and abstract concepts, the gender of the noun is arbitrary.

  Masculine: *tiburón* (shark), *buitre* (vulture), *salmón* (salmon), *virus* (virus), *pupitre* (desk), *sofá* (sofa), *bolígrafo* (ball pen), *abrigo* (coat), *amor* (love), *caos* (chaos).

  Feminine: *ballena* (whale), *águila* (eagle), *trucha* (trout), *bacteria* (bacteria), *mesa* (table), *silla* (chair), *pluma* (fountain pen), *capa* (cloak), *pasión* (passion), *nada* (nothing).

1. Tag the following words as feminine or masculine.

1. Presión ➠ **F**
2. Negra ➠ _____
3. Mujer ➠ _____
4. Amor ➠ _____
5. Verde ➠ _____

2. Provide the other gender of the following nouns.

1. Padre   *Madre*
2. Escritor   _____
3. Alumno   _____
4. Grande   _____
5. Pequeña   _____

3. Form 'noun + adjective' sequences by joining words from both columns.

1. Hombre   a) sencillo
2. Vaca   b) inteligente
3. Lápiz   c) gorda
4. Abuela   d) gris
5. Poema   e) buena

4. Correct the following sentences if necessary:

1. Rosa es mi profesor de matemáticas. ➠ *Rosa es mi profesora de matemáticas.*
2. Pedro es una chica muy inteligente. _____
3. Mi madre se llama Miguel. _____
4. Mi amiga Cristina es guapo. _____
5. El payaso es muy divertida. _____

7 IS IT A BOY OR A GIRL?
THE GENDER OF NOUNS

- In order to distinguish between males and females in less familiar animals, it is possible to append the nouns *macho* (male) or *hembra* (female).

    un tiburón hembra (a female shark)

    un tiburón macho (a male shark)

    una ballena hembra (a female whale)

    una ballena macho (a male whale)

- There are devices to state the gender of other ambiguous nouns in the few cases where there is not a masculine or feminine noun. For example, the noun *mujer* or *hombre* precedes some professions. In most other cases, the adjectives *masculino* or *femenino* can follow.

    mujer policía (policewoman)

    modelo masculino (male model)

- A clue in order to find out the gender of a given noun is to look at its ending. Most nouns that finish in **-o** (and also: **-án, -e, -és, -ón, -or**) are masculine, and most nouns that finish in **-a** (and also: **-ie, -ión, -iz, -dad, -tad, -tud, -umbre**) are feminine.

MASCULINE	FEMININE
*american**o*** (American man)	*australian**a*** (Australian woman)
*gall**o*** (cock)	*gallin**a*** (hen)
*coraz**ón*** (heart)	*pas**ión*** (passion)
*pescad**or*** (fisherman)	*actr**iz*** (actress)
*comed**or*** (dining room)	*perd**iz*** (partridge)
*tamb**or*** (drum)	*libert**ad*** (freedom)

- However, there are several exceptions to these rules, so it is advisable to learn new Spanish words together with their gender.

MASCULINE	FEMININE
idioma (language)	*mano* (hand)
aprendiz (apprentice)	*labor* (task)
pie (foot)	*madre* (mother)
avión (airplane)	*calle* (street)

5. Provide the other gender of the following nouns (use a dictionary if necessary).

1. Jirafa hembra ➡ *Jirafa hembra.*

2. Gallina _____

3. Leopardo macho _____

4. Caballo _____

5. Gato _____

6. Translate into Spanish.

1. The English woman ➡ *La mujer inglesa.*

2. The pretty doll ➡ _____

3. The yellow car ➡ _____

4. The terrible day ➡ _____

5. The beautiful night ➡ _____

7. Make whatever changes are necessary to form correct sentences leaving the verbs intact.

1. Las grande cantantes cantan hoy. ➡ *Las grandes cantantes cantan hoy.*

2. El árbol alta tiene flores. _____

3. Transportamos los botellas enormes. _____

4. Comemos el pollo pequeñas. _____

5. La atleta veloz aparece en la televisión. _____

8. Complete with the correct ending (-o, -or, -iz, -a, -e, -és).

1. Italian____ (Italian man)

2. Emperatr____ (empress)

3. Monj____ (monk)

4. Leon____ (lioness)

5. Pint____ (male painter)

6. Doctor____ (female doctor)

7. Holand____ (Dutchman)

8. Gat____ (male cat)

8 ONE SUGAR OR TWO SUGARS?
SINGULAR AND PLURAL

- Nouns are singular when they refer to a single entity, and plural when they refer to more than one. In this case, **-s** is generally added if the noun ends in a vowel, and **-es** if it ends in a consonant.

- Forming some plurals can entail some spelling change (e.g., **z-** does not appear before **-e**, it changes to **c-**).

un cepillo (a/one brush)	*dos cepillos* (two brushes)
un jabón (a/one soap)	*dos jabones* (two soaps)
una voz (a/one voice)	*dos voces* (two voices)

- If a noun is collective, i.e., it refers to a group of items, the standard plural can still generally be formed.

ganado /ganados (cattle)	*olivar /olivares* (olive grove)
gobierno /gobiernos (government)	*familia /familias* (families)

- Beware of the fact that a small percentage of nouns do not have the same number in English and Spanish, e.g., *horca* (gallows) is singular, not plural.

- Also, in Spanish there is no flexibility when using a plural verb with a singular collective noun like in British English.

  El equipo es líder de la liga este año (The team are leaders of the league this year).

- Some words of Latin and classic Greek origin ending in **-s** do not alter their form in the plural.

  caos (chaos)   *virus* (virus)

1. Provide the plurals of the following words.

1. Tesis ➠ *Tesis.*

2. Sarampión ➠ _____

3. Lluvia ➠ _____

4. Tifus ➠ _____

5. Comité ➠ _____

2. Provide the singular forms of the following words.

1. Ciudades ➠ *Ciudad.*

2. Países ➠ _____

3. Mimos ➠ _____

4. Raíces ➠ _____

5. Vacaciones ➠ _____

3. Rewrite the following sentences, pluralizing every word.

1. Yo regalo un reloj. ➠ *Nosotros regalamos unos relojes.*

2. Tú plantas un árbol. _____

3. Él riega un jardín. _____

4. Ella conduce un autobús. _____

5. El niño tiene un virus. _____

4. Rewrite the following sentences, putting every possible word in singular.

1. Las niñas comen las manzanas. ➠ *La niña come la manzana.*

2. Los virus están en los laboratorios.

   _____

3. Ellos cultivan muchos tomates.

   _____

4. Los alumnos estudian para los exámenes.

   _____

5. Los edificios de los centros de las ciudades son los más altos.

   _____

ONE SUGAR OR TWO SUGARS?
SINGULAR AND PLURAL

- It can also be the case that a noun referring to a single entity is plural, normally because it has a multiple constitution. In this case the number of units is indicated by means of a number and preferably a phrase like *par de* (pair of).

    unas gafas /un par de gafas (a pair of glasses)

    dos gafas /dos pares de gafas (two pairs of glasses)

    unos pantalones /un par de pantalones (a pair of trousers)

    dos pantalones /dos pares de pantalones (two pairs of trousers)

- There are many nouns that take that type of phrase, like *periodo de* (period of), *filete de* (slice of, fillet of), *kilo de* (kilo of), etc. Again, there are nouns that can be counted in one of the languages, and not the other.

    unas vacaciones /un periodo de vacaciones (a holiday period)

    dos vacaciones /dos periodos de vacaciones (two holiday periods)

    una fruta /una pieza de fruta (a piece of fruit)

    dos frutas /dos piezas de fruta (two pieces of fruit)

    una noticia (one piece of news)

    dos noticias (two pieces of news)

- Abstract nouns can be singular or plural in form, but they cannot generally be counted, so they do not show two forms for singular and plural. The alternative, if possible, often implies a difference in the meaning:

    *matemática /matemáticas (mathematics)

    generosidad (generosity) /**generosidades*

    imaginación (imagination)/*imaginaciones* (fantasies)

    amistad (friendship)/*amistades* (friends)

- The plural of *persona* (person) can be confusing. In Spanish there are two plural forms (two equivalents of 'people'): *personas*, which is countable and hence emphasizes individuality, and *gente*, which cannot be counted and refers to the group. The former is grammatically plural (it takes a plural article, verb, etc.) and the second, singular.

    Dos personas esperan fuera (Two people are waiting outside).

    Observo a la gente atónita /Observo a las personas atónitas (I look at the astonished people).

    La gente de este país es amable /Las personas de este país son amables (People in this country are kind).

5. Match fragments from the two columns below.

1. La decisión   a) trabajan en un banco.
2. Los equipos de waterpolo   b) es muy importante.
3. Sonia y Jaime   c) corre dos kilómetros todas las mañanas.
4. El policía   d) viste un uniforme azul.
5. Arturo   e) entrenan todos los días.

6. Select the most suitable plural of *persona* for each sentence below, adding the suitable article and conjugating the verb in brackets accordingly when necessary.

1. *Las personas tienen* (tener) buen corazón.
2. Hay (there are) millones de _____ enamoradas (in love).
3. Hablo con (with) _____ _____ implicadas (involved).
4. _____ _____ en (in) España _____ (comer) cordero en Navidad.
5. _____ _____ _____ (expresar) distintas opiniones en las elecciones.

7. Make a sentence from the following fragments of information, writing the numbers in full.

1. Manuel y yo / planear / 2 / vacaciones de verano (summer holidays).
   Manuel y yo planeamos dos periodos de vacaciones de verano.
2. Luis y Susana / comprar / 5 / prismáticos.
   _____
3. Las modistas / usar / 93 / tijeras.
   _____
4. La lavadora / lavar / 25 / pantalones.
   _____
5. El carnicero / cortar / 5 / carne.
   _____

8. Translate the following sentences into Spanish.

1. We buy a new pair of glasses for the summer.
   Nosotros compramos un nuevo par de gafas para el verano.
2. María has lots of friends. _____
3. There are a lot of people at the restaurant. _____
4. This person is very interesting. _____
5. I need a loaf of bread. _____

9 LA NIÑA BONITA

WORD ORDER

- Short words like titles, articles, demonstratives, possessives and numbers typically precede nouns, while most adjectives and complex modifiers follow them.

  Estos dos perritos alegres y juguetones (these two jolly and playful doggies).

  El ordenador último modelo (the latest model computer).

- There are a few adjectives that can appear before the noun, e.g., *nuevo* (new) and *old* (viejo), *bueno* (good) and *malo* (bad), *grande* (big) and *pequeño* (small). In some cases the position entails a change of meaning: the preceding adjective only modifies the aspect of the entity denoted by the noun (for example, the fact that he or she is a student), not the whole entity (the whole human being who, among other things, studies).

  Una esposa buena (a wife who is good in general).

  Una buena esposa (somebody who is good in her role as a wife).

  Un amigo viejo (a friend of old age).

  Un viejo amigo (somebody who has been a friend for a long time).

  Un hombre grande (a man who is tall and well-built).

  Un gran hombre (a man who is exceptional) (note the change in form).

- There are adjectives that change their masculine singular form if they appear before the noun. In the case of *grande* (big), *gran* is used for masculine and singular.

  Un buen sitio – un sitio bueno (a good place).

  Un mal sueño – un sueño malo (a bad dream).

  Un gran proyecto (an important proyect) – *un proyecto grande* (a big project).

ES MI GRAN AMIGA.

1. Complete the following phrases by adding the equivalent adjectives in brackets in the right form and position.

   1. Un **mal** compañero (bad).

   2. Unas _____ vecinas (bad).

   3. Una _____ razón (good).

   4. Un _____ castigo (good).

   5. Unos _____ almacenes (big).

2. Match words from each of the three columns.

1. Las	payasos	grises
2. Los	chicas	viejo
3. El	casa	delgadas
4. La	elefantes	divertidos
5. Los	ordenador	de madera

3. Reorder the following words to form coherent and correct phrases.

   1. libros / tres / los / clásicos / interesantes ➠ *Los tres libros clásicos interesantes.*

   2. historia / una / triste / romántica

   _____

   3. profesor / el / jubilado / de matemáticas ➠ _____

   _____

   4. monjas / algunas / buenas / pacientes ➠ _____

   _____

   5. amigos / algunos / cubanos / íntimos ➠ _____

   _____

4. Translate the following sentences into Spanish.

   1. The three good friends. ➠ *Los tres buenos amigos. / Las tres buenas amigas.*

   2. A beautiful and healthy baby. ➠ _____

   3. Two dry and thirsty plants. ➠ _____

   4. A fast cyclist. ➠ _____

   5. A million red balloons. ➠ _____

9 *LA NIÑA BONITA*
WORD ORDER

- The majority of masculine adjectives end in **-o** and feminine ones end in **-a**; others, like most colours, do not vary. In cases of invariable nouns and adjectives, determiners are crucial to clarify gender.

  un *brujo malvado* (a wicked wizard)
  una *bruja malvada* (a wicked witch)

  un *señor inteligente* (an intelligent gentleman)
  una *señora inteligente* (an intelligent lady)

  un *policía valiente* (a brave policeman)
  una *policía valiente* (a brave policewoman)

  un *periodista tenaz* (a tenacious male journalist)
  una *periodista tenaz* (a tenacious female journalist)

- When there is more than one modifier in the phrase, the same ordering principle as in English is followed: the most significant adjectives are closest to the word they modify – but on its right.

  For example, if an adjective is modifying another (as in 'pale yellow paper') the modifying adjective appears behind the modified one *(papel amarillo pálido)*.

- Adjectives that add the same type of content (e.g., physical features, measurements, etc.) may be separated by commas or **y** (and) before the last one.

  *Una niña alta **y** rubia* (a tall and blonde girl).

  Un coche deportivo amarillo (a yellow sports car).

  *Un bloque grande, pesado **y** de hormigón* (a big, heavy concrete block) (**de** introduces matter).

5. Put the correct form of the equivalent word or words in brackets.

1. Una caja (big and yellow). ➡ *Una caja grande y amarilla.*

2. Un amigo (generous). ➡ _____

3. Un examen (long). ➡ _____

4. Unas vacaciones (relaxed). ➡ _____

5. Una situación (complicated). ➡ _____

6. Join the phrases in the column on the left with the paraphrases in the column on the right.

1. Un regalo pequeño.	a) A caring, loving brother.
2. Un pequeño regalo.	b) A brother who is physically big.
3. Un hermano grande.	c) A student who is a nasty person.
4. Un gran hermano.	d) A student who does not work hard enough, obtains insufficient results, etc.
5. Un estudiante malo.	e) A present which does not occupy much space.
6. Un mal estudiante.	f) A little something as a present.

7. Make Spanish phrases that mean the following.

1. A ball which is dark blue. ➡ *Una pelota azul oscuro.*

2. A statue which is dark and tall. ➡ _____

3. A hammer which is hard and made of wood. ➡ _____

4. The French vegetarian high cuisine. ➡ _____

5. A tall bold German singer. ➡ _____

8. Make whatever corrections you consider necessary in the following sentences.

1. Escucho a una escritor magnífica. ➡ *Escucho a una escritora magnífica.*

2. Arreglo un gran radio. _____

3. Contratamos payasos alegros. _____

4. Abres una puerta marrón. _____

5. Las estudiantes jóvenes bailen. _____

I STUDY SPANISH
USES OF THE PRESENT TENSE

- In unit 3 we saw the conjugation for the simple present tense. Let us now see the uses of this tense.

- The present tense is used for timeless statements, permanent or long lasting states, and habitual, regular or repeated actions.

  *Los perros **tienen** cuatro patas* (Dogs have four legs).

  *La Tierra **gira** alrededor del Sol* (The Earth rotates around the Sun).

  *Siempre **como** en la universidad* (I always eat at university).

VIVO EN SEGOVIA.

- A highly common verb used to introduce habitual (not necessarily regular) actions is *soler,* which precedes an infinitive (the verb referring to the action ending in **-ar, -er,** or **-ir**). *Soler* is a rather irregular verb:

  ***Suelo** ir al cine los lunes. = Normalmente voy al cine los lunes.* (I usually go to the cinema on Mondays.)

  ***Sueles** comer a las dos. = Normalmente comes a las dos.* (You usually eat at two.)

  ***Suele** trabajar hasta las 5. = Normalmente trabaja hasta las 5.* (He usually works till 5.)

  ***Solemos** jugar al fútbol. = Normalmente jugamos al fútbol.* (We usually play football.)

  ***Soléis** esperar al autobús del colegio. = Normalmente esperáis al autobús del colegio.* (You usually wait for the school bus.)

  ***Suelen** ayudar a su madre. = Normalmente ayudan a su madre.* (They usually help their mum.)

1. In the sentences below, decide if the verb refers to something permanent (P) or to something habitual (H).

1. Siempre vamos de vacaciones en el mes de agosto. H

2. A los gatos les gusta el pescado. _____

3. La cenas que prepara suelen estar deliciosas. _____

4. María suele estudiar en la biblioteca. _____

5. Yo vivo en Madrid. _____

2. Correct the following sentences of timeless truths and regular actions.

1. Arañas tiene las seis patas. ➡ *Las arañas tienen seis patas.*

2. Las luces viajen a (at) grande velocidad.

   _____

3. La semana tiene algunos siete días.

   _____

4. Nuria y Mónica fuma unos cigarrillos.

   _____

5. Niños juegan con (with) balones y otros (others) con soldados.

   _____

3. Fill out the following gaps with a suitable verb.

1. Las ranas *croan / saltan* sobre (on) los nenúfares.

2. La mona _____ un coco con una piedra.

3. La ballena _____ en el mar.

4. Los leones _____ en manadas.

5. Los mosquitos _____ en verano.

4. Translate the following sentences about habitual actions into Spanish in two different ways.

1. You usually do your homework with Teresa.

   Sueles hacer tus deberes con Teresa. / Normalmente haces tus deberes con Teresa.

2. Birds usually make nests on *(en)* trees.

   _____

3. I usually film the children on the beach.

   _____

4. She usually cooks meals for *(para)* the whole *(toda la)* week.

   _____

5. The dog usually barks at the postman.

   _____

I STUDY SPANISH
USES OF THE PRESENT TENSE

- One of the different uses of the Spanish simple present with respect to English is spontaneous speech. It is convenient to learn these somewhat idiomatic expressions by heart:

    *¡**Llaman** a la puerta!* (Someone is ringing the doorbell!).

    *Cuidado, **viene** un coche* (Be careful, there is a car coming).

    ***Tengo** mucha hambre* (I'm starving).

- The simple present can be used for highly likely future actions such as officially timetabled events and short-term intentions.

    *Mi tren **sale** a las siete* (My train leaves at seven).

    *La semana que viene **jugamos** contra el vencedor* (Next week we play against the winner).

    ***Vuelve** enseguida* (He'll be right back).

- The simple present can also be used for the past in historical narrative.

    *Colón **parte** de Palos el 3 de agosto de 1492.*
    (Columbus left from Palos on August 3rd 1492.)

    *Picasso **nace** en una familia de clase media.*
    (Picasso was born in a middle class family.)

    *Pedro Almodóvar **gana** su segundo Óscar.*
    (Pedro Almodóvar won his second Oscar.)

- Finally, it can express events that started in the past and are still going on:

    ***Vivimos** en Barcelona desde enero.*
    (We have lived in Barcelona since January.)

    ***Estudia** parapsicología desde 1978.*
    (He has been studying parapsychology since 1978.)

    ***Es** una persona muy alegre desde siempre.*
    (He has always been a very jolly person.)

- When followed by a time reference, 'have/has been' is usually translated by *llevar* (literally, 'to take with someone, to carry') in the simple present, rather than by *estar* (to be) (see unit 11).

    ***Llevo** una hora en la esquina* (I have been on the corner for an hour).

    ***Lleva** en Madrid toda la vida* (He has been in Madrid all his life).

5. Conjugate the verb in the simple present for the following spontaneous expressions.

1. Me **muero** (morir) por visitar Disneylandia (I'm dying to visit Disneyland).

2. Cuidado, que te _____ (ver) (Be careful; I'm watching you).

3. _____ (tocar) a la puerta (Somebody's knocking at the door).

4. _____ (ir) a la tienda un momento (I'm going to the shop for a minute).

5. ¿_____ (venir)? ¡Nos _____ (ir) ya! (Are you coming? We're going now!).

6. Translate the following sentences into Spanish.

1. He works in a big oil company. ➡ **Él trabaja en una gran compañía petrolífera.**

2. The royal family stays in Majorca in August.

   _____

3. They dance salsa like (como) Brazilians.

   _____

4. We practise sports in our (nuestro) free time.

   _____

5. Astronauts follow a strict diet.

   _____

7. Indicate if the actions referred to in the following sentences are timeless or take place in the past, in the present, or in the future.

1. La Luna gira alrededor (around) del Sol. _____

2. Su avión llega a las cuatro. _____

3. Leo Pister recibe un premio en Berlín a los (at the age of) cuarenta años. _____

4. Trabajamos como (as) enfermeras desde nuestra graduación. _____

5. Recibe clases de ballet los sábados. _____

8. Translate the following sentences into English with the corresponding logical tense.

1. La niñera lleva a los niños al colegio. ➡ **The nanny takes the children to school.**

2. Mi familia lleva viviendo en Galicia muchos años.

   _____

3. Tus sobrinos llevan los libros en sus mochilas.

   _____

4. Carlos lleva esperando a Susana una hora.

   _____

5. Lleva lloviendo toda la semana.

   _____

11 SER OR ESTAR, THAT IS THE QUESTION
THE VERBS SER AND ESTAR

- In Spanish there are two equivalent verbs of to be: *ser* and *estar*. Below is their present tense.

SER		ESTAR	
Yo	soy	Yo	estoy
Tú	eres	Tú	estás
Él/ella	es	Él/ella	está
Nosotros/as	somos	Nosotros/as	estamos
Vosotros/as	sois	Vosotros/as	estáis
Ellos/as	son	Ellos/as	están

- *Ser* is used for more or less permanent and inherent conditions, with no suggestion of change:

   Soy mujer (I am a woman).

   Eres de Sevilla (You come from Seville).

- Conversely, *estar* introduces a temporary feature or state which is not expected to last too long:

   Estamos de vacaciones (We are on holidays).

   Estáis cansadas (You are tired).

1. Complete the sentences below with the suitable form of *ser*.

1. María *es* muy generosa.
2. Nosotros _____ unos chicos tranquilos.
3. Tú _____ mi novio.
4. Vosotros _____ profesores en la universidad.
5. Arturo y Federico _____ muy buenos estudiantes.

2. Now do the same with the verb *estar*.

1. Vosotras *estáis* en el hotel.
2. La ventanas no _____ rotas.
3. La manzana _____ verde (meaning 'unripe', not 'green').
4. Juan _____ muy cansado.
5. Ellos _____ a punto de llegar.

3. Answer the following questions with full sentences.

1. ¿Estás trabajando en Iberia? ➡ *Sí, estoy trabajando en Iberia.*
2. ¿Sois hermanos? No, _____
3. ¿No estáis cómodas? Sí, _____
4. ¿Soy su secretaria? Sí, _____
5. ¿Estoy gordo? No, _____

4. Complete the sentences below by selecting a suitable complement from the box.

> sorprendida – miembros de Greenpeace – de oro – Elena – en casa
> mi padre – el 25 de julio de 1965 – nueve – algo nerviosa

1. Todos somos *miembros de Greenpeace.*
2. No son _____
3. Cinco y cuatro son _____
4. Aquella señora no es _____
5. Soy / estoy _____
6. Isabel, éste es _____
7. Mi fecha de nacimiento es _____
8. Estamos _____
9. Mi prima está _____

11

SER OR *ESTAR*, THAT IS THE QUESTION
THE VERBS *SER* AND *ESTAR*

- Most adjectives can be used with *ser* or *estar*, and in some cases their meaning may vary.

    Es *delgado* (He is thin by constitution).

    Está *delgado* (He has lost weight lately).

    Soy *feliz* (I am generally satisfied with my life).

    Estoy *feliz* (I feel cheerful right now).

    Es *guapa* (She is naturally pretty).

    Está *guapa* (She looks pretty now).

    Las peras **son** *verdes* (The colour of the pears is green).

    Las peras **están** *verdes* (The pears are unripe).

- Sometimes the change in the use of *ser* or *estar* corresponds to the use of the endings **-ing** or **-ed** in the adjective:

    Son *aburridos* (They are boring). – **Están** *aburridos* (They are bored).

    Es *confuso* (It is confusing). – **Está** *confundido* (It is confused).

    Eres *sorprendente* (You are surprising). – **Estás** *sorprendido* (You are surprised).

- In order to help you decide between *ser* and *estar*, try and rephrase the English sentence adding 'in a xxx state' at the end. If you can, use *estar* for the Spanish.

    – He is pleased: ... *contento*. ➡ He is in a pleased state: *Está contento*.

    – She is rich: ... *rica*. ➡ *She is in a rich state: *Es rica*.

- Apart from the above, there are set expressions that always require *ser* or *estar*, regardless of their temporal quality.

    POSSESSION: *Esta oportunidad* **es** *mía* (This opportunity is mine).

    ORIGIN: **Somos** *de las Islas Canarias* (We are from the Canary Islands).

    THE TIME: *¿Qué hora* **es**? **Son** *las tres y media* (What time is it? It's half past three).

    LOCATION: *Este cuadro* **está** *en el museo desde 1915* (This picture has been in the museum since 1915).

    CONTINUOUS ACTION: **Están** *buscando la tumba desde hace años* (They have been looking for the tomb for years).

5. Join each sentence in Spanish with its best equivalent in English.

1. Estoy sorda.   a) They are clever.
2. Soy sorda.   b) He is not handsome.
3. Son listos.   c) He doesn't look handsome today.
4. Están listos.   d) I can't hear very well right now.
5. No es guapo.   e) I am deaf.
6. No está guapo.   f) They are ready.

6. Correct the following sentences, making changes in the verbs if necessary.

1. Estamos fans de Julio Iglesias. ➡ *Somos fans de Julio Iglesias.*

2. Soy amigo de mis amigos. _____

3. El turno está de Lola. _____

4. No somos en Buenos Aires. _____

5. Son comiendo en un restaurante. _____

7. Match the two columns to create a sentence.

1. Su hija está   a) muy larga.
2. Los tomates están   b) unas trabajadoras responsables.
3. Ellas son   c) cerrada con llave.
4. La puerta está   d) muy alta.
5. La película es   e) caros.

8. Translate the following sentences into Spanish.

1. My friends are Canadian. ➡ *Mis amigos son canadienses.*

2. I am very tired. _____

3. We are delighted to see you. _____

4. She is a very pleasant girl. _____

5. This film is very boring. _____

12 TIME FLIES LIKE THIS LESSON

ASKING AND TELLING THE TIME

- The standard way to ask for the time in Spanish is: *¿Qué hora es?* (What time is it?). Of course, you may add *por favor* (please) at some point of such questions to sound more polite.

- There are, however, other more or less formal expressions:

    ¿Podría decirme, por favor, la hora? (Could you please tell me the time?)

    ¿Tienes hora? (Have you got the time?)

- The standard way to tell the time in Spanish is similar to English in that it is established on a twelve-hour, five-minute basis. However, it involves a difference in the relative order of hours and minutes which is reversed:

    Las once y cinco (Five past eleven).

    Las cuatro menos veinticinco (Twenty-five to four).

- Other differences are:

Las tres (three o'clock; 'o'clock' is understood when nothing follows the hour).

Las tres y diez (ten past three).

Las tres menos veinte (twenty to three).

Las tres y media (half past three).

Las tres y cuarto (a quarter past three).

Las tres menos cuarto (a quarter to three).

1. Match the two columns below.

a) 2.10   Las doce menos cuarto.

b) 5.25   Las seis en punto.

c) 7.50   Las cinco y veinticinco.

d) 6.00   Las dos y diez.

e) 11.45   Las ocho menos diez.

2. Express the following time information numerically.

1. Las cuatro y veinte. ➠ *4.20*

2. La una y cinco. ➠ _____

3. Las doce y cuarto. ➠ _____

4. Las once y veinticinco. ➠ _____

5. Las tres y media. ➠ _____

3. Draw the following time by adding the hands to the clock faces.

Las cuatro menos veinte.   La una menos cinco.   Las doce menos cuarto.

Las dos.   Las once menos veinticinco.   Las cinco y media.

4. What time is it?

a) 1.00   *Es la una.*

b) 2.05   _____

c) 3.10   _____

d) 4.15   _____

e) 5.20   _____

f) 6.30   _____

g) 7.35   _____

h) 8.40   _____

i) 9.45   _____

j) 10.50   _____

12

TIME FLIES LIKE THIS LESSON
ASKING AND TELLING THE TIME

- Note that the words *minuto(s)* and *hora(s)* are omitted when telling the time. However, since the latter is a feminine noun, the corresponding number is preceded by *la /las* (depending on whether it is 'one' or any other).

    ***Las** diez y cinco* (five past ten).

    ***La** una menos cuarto* (a quarter to one).

- *En punto* is used to emphasize the exactness of the time, e.g., *son las cuatro y media en punto* (it's exactly half four), and it is particularly common with the exact hours, e.g., *son las once en punto* (it's eleven o'clock).

- You can introduce the sentence with the verb *es* (singular) or *son* (plural), particularly when you are announcing the time rather than answering a question (the choice between *es* and *son* also depends on whether it is the first hour or any other):

    ***Es** la una y veinte* (It's twenty past one).

    ***Son** las siete menos cuarto* (It's a quarter to seven).

- When telling the time the Latin locutions 'ante meridiem' / 'post meridiem' (or 'a.m.' / 'p.m.') are not used. Rather the expressions *de la mañana* (before lunch), *de la tarde* (after lunch) and *de la noche* (usually after 9 p.m.) are used. For the latter, the exact time may vary according to the speaker or other criteria such as the time of the year (if it is dark at eight p.m. in winter, you may refer to it as *las ocho de la noche*, 'eight o'clock at night'). Note that the preposition is always *de*:

    Son las diez de la mañana (It's ten a.m.).

    Es la una de la mañana (It's one a.m.).

    Son las once de la noche (It's eleven p.m.).

    Son las tres de la tarde (It's three p.m.).

- *Mediodía* can be used for the hours between twelve a.m. and lunch time (in Spain around two p.m.) and *medianoche* is another word for twelve p.m.:

    Nos vemos a la una del mediodía (See you at one p.m.).

    Es medianoche (It's midnight).

- Finally, *madrugada* may be used instead of *mañana* for the early hours of the day.

    El camión de la basura pasa a las dos de la madrugada (The dustbin lorry comes by at two in the morning).

5. Translate the following time information and write it numerically.

1. It's twenty to five. ➡ *Son las cinco menos veinte. – 4.40.*

2. It's half past twelve. ➡ _____

3. It's twenty-five past nine. ➡ _____

4. It's a quarter to seven. ➡ _____

5. It's eleven o'clock. ➡ _____

6. Correct the following sentences if necessary.

1. Es las diez. ➡ *Son las diez.*

2. ¿Qué horas son? Son las tres y cuarto.

_____

3. ¿Me dice la hora, por favor? Las cuatro menos veinticinco.

_____

4. Son las tres menos media.

_____

5. ¿Tienes la hora? Son la una y diez.

_____

7. Answer the following questions, especifying *de la mañana / tarde / noche*.

1. ¿A qué hora desayunas? (8.00 a.m.) ➡ *Desayuno a las ocho de la mañana.*

2. ¿A qué hora comes? (1.30 p.m.) _____

3. ¿A qué hora meriendas? (6.15 p.m.) _____

4. ¿A qué hora cenas? (8.45 p.m.) _____

5. ¿A qué hora vuelves? (3.00 a.m.) _____

8. Translate the following sentences.

1. It's a quarter to seven. ➡ *Son las siete menos cuarto.*

2. What time does the train arrive? _____

3. The plane lands at half past four. _____

4. They finish at nine p.m. _____

5. I wake up at half past six a.m. _____

13 ARE YOU COMING OR GOING?
PREPOSITIONS OF PLACE AND MOVEMENT

HOY ES EL 12 DE OCTUBRE DE 1492. ESTOY EN AMÉRICA.

- Prepositions may consist of one word (e.g., *en*, *de*) or more than one word (e.g., *junto a, en frente de*). The most general preposition used in Spanish to indicate location is **en**, no matter whether it is a continent, a country, a region, a city, a street or your sofa.

    *Vivís **en** Sevilla* (You live in Seville).

    *Dormimos **en** esta cama* (We sleep in this bed).

    *Estoy **en** el dentista* (I am at the dentist).

    *Trabajas **en** una granja* (You work on a farm).

- There are other prepositions to indicate positions with respect to a given site. Beware of exceptions like *dormir en el suelo* (to sleep on the floor) and *ir de vacaciones* (to go on holidays), and of the false friend: *en frente de*, which is not equivalent to 'in front of', but to 'opposite'.

    *El libro está **sobre / encima de** la mesa* (The book is on the table).

    *Los zapatos están **bajo / debajo de** la cama* (The shoes are under the bed).

    *La estación está **en frente de** la iglesia* (The station is opposite the church).

    *La señora está **delante del** señor* (The lady is in front of the gentleman).

    *El señor está **detrás de** la señora* (The gentleman is behind the lady).

    *Las niñas comen **al lado de** sus padres* (The girls eat beside their parents).

    *Mallorca está **cerca de** Menorca* (Majorca is near Minorca).

    *Ibiza está **lejos de** Groenlandia* (Eivissa is far from Groenland).

- In order to express movement, the preposition **por** must be added in front of the prepositions above, except *sobre, bajo, al lado de, cerca de, lejos de,* which remain the same.

    *El avión vuela **por debajo del** puente* (The plane flies under the bridge).

    *El barco navega **lejos de** la costa* (The ship sails far from the coast).

1. Fill out the gaps with a suitable preposition.

1. El coche rojo gana la carrera. Está *delante de* los demás (the rest).

2. La sábana suele estar _____ el edredón.

3. Trabajo _____ un despacho.

4. No veo bien a Lourdes porque (because) estoy _____ ella.

5. Pedro está escondido _____ la puerta.

2. Match the following pairs of opposites.

1. encima de   a) cerca de

2. delante de   b) sobre

3. lejos de   c) debajo de

4. bajo   d) de espaldas a

5. frente a   e) detrás de

3. Make sentences in Spanish out of the following chunks.

1. Los cubiertos / estar / la mesa.

   Los cubiertos están sobre / encima de la mesa.

2. La mesa / estar / el mantel.

   _____

3. El cliente / dejar / el vaso / el plato.

   _____

4. El camarero / poner / el tenedor / la cuchara.

   _____

5. El pan / estar / la mantequilla.

   _____

4. Put the prepositions in brackets in the right position in each sentence:

1. Juan y María viajan *en* coche *a* Madrid. (a / en)

2. Mis amigos viven _____ mis padres _____ Barcelona. (cerca de / en)

3. La caja está _____ la mesa y _____ la pizarra. (cerca de / encima de)

4. La muñeca está _____ la puerta _____ la caja. (dentro de / detrás de)

5. Sonia _____ la playa se sienta _____ las rocas. (lejos de / en)

13

ARE YOU COMING OR GOING?
PREPOSITIONS OF PLACE AND MOVEMENT

- The most common preposition to express direction towards a destination is *a*. It often appears with the verb *ir* (to go) or *llegar* (to arrive). Since *ir* is an irregular verb, below is its simple present. Remember that *a + el* always contracts to *al*, just like *de + el* contracts to *del* (see unit 2). *Entrar* (to go in, to enter) takes *en*.

    Voy a *Bilbao* (I go to Bilbao).

    Vas a *la cama* (You go to bed).

    Va a *una boda* (He/She goes to a wedding).

    Vamos al *colegio* (We go to school).

    Vais a *comer* (You go to eat / for a meal).

    Van a *la ópera* (They go to the opera).

- The omission of the article in some English expressions of habitual actions does not necessarily occur in Spanish (e.g., *ir a clase* [go to class], *ir a misa* [go to church], *ir a la universidad* [go to university]).

- If you want to indicate only the direction, but not necessarily the destination, the preposition is **hacia**. Conversely, if you want to emphasize the last point you reach, the preposition is **hasta**.

    Cabalgo **hacia** *Madrid* (I ride towards Madrid).

    Nadas **hasta** *el faro* (You swim as far as the lighthouse).

    Nadamos **hacia** *el norte* (We swim towards the north).

    Corren **hasta** *el autobús* (They ran up to the bus).

- The starting point of the destination is introduced by **de**, whether you are coming or leaving. In the former case, it often follows verbs like *venir* (to come) or *volver* (to return); in the latter, verbs like *salir* (to go out, to leave) and *partir* (to depart). In order to emphasize the starting point, the preposition used is **desde**.

    Vengo **de** *la peluquería* (I come from the hairdresser's).

    Sale **de** *su casa* (He leaves his house).

    Parten **desde** *el puerto* (They depart from the harbour).

    Vuelves **de** *un viaje* (You return from a trip).

5. Complete the sentences with the correct form *(a la, al, de la, del).*

1. Sergio va **al** cine.
2. El doctor sale _____ consulta.
3. Mis amigos van _____ playa.
4. Yo vengo con mi madre _____ colegio.
5. Vamos _____ supermercado temprano esta mañana.

6. Translate the following sentences:

1. I come from the department stores. ➥ *Vengo de los grandes almacenes.*
2. They fly from Paris every weekend.

   _____

3. The packets are near the fireplace.

   _____

4. They walk to the end of the road.

   _____

5. She runs towards the baby.

   _____

7. Select a suitable word, adding whatever other words are necessary to complete each of the sentences below.

```
mar – cine – guardería – clase – trabajar
```

1. La profesora trabaja *en una / la guardería.*
2. El salmón nada _____
3. Vamos _____
4. Venimos _____
5. Los estudiantes están _____

8. Make corrections to the following sentences if necessary.

1. Son las ocho. Vas a la oficina a trabajar. _____
2. Son las once. Va a un reunión a tomar notas (take notes). _____
3. Son las dos y cuarto. Vais a el restaurante a comer. _____
4. Son las cinco y media. Voy a la casa a descansar. _____
5. Son las once. Vamos a cama a dormir. _____

14 LET'S MAKE FUNNY NOISES
SOME LETTERS AND THEIR SOUNDS

- As seen in unit 1, there are a few Spanish letters that do not have a one-to-one correspondence to a sound in English. Therefore, the words that contain them need special attention on the part of the learner.

- **B / V.** They are both pronounced like the English 'b'. There are a few similar words spelt with one or the other (e.g., *baca* is 'roof rack' and *vaca*, 'cow'). This means that deciding between them for a given word cannot be deduced from the word's pronunciation so it must be memorized. There are a few particular words that may be hard to learn because of the difference between both languages.

> *go**b**ierno* (go**v**ernment)
> *mó**v**il* (mo**b**ile)
> *ta**b**erna* (ta**v**ern)
> *sa**b**ana* (sa**v**annah)

There are two spelling rules involving 'b': 'b' can appear before 'r' or 'l', but not 'v', and 'm' can appear before 'b' or 'p', but not 'n'.

> *ha**bl**ar* (to speak)
> *ca**br**a* (goat)
> *ca**mb**io* (change)
> *ca**mp**o* (field)

- **LL / Y.** They are both pronounced like the English 'y' in words like 'young' and 'yours'. There are also a few similar words spelt with one or the other.

> *po**ll**o* (chicken)   *po**y**o* (stone bench)
> *ha**ll**a* (he finds)   *ha**y**a* (beech tree)
> *ca**ll**ó* (he kept quiet)   *ca**y**ó* (he fell)
> *va**ll**a* (fence)   *ba**y**a* (berry)

1. Correct the 'b' and the 'v' in the following sentences if necessary.

  1. Ésta es mi taverna preferida. ➡ *Ésta es mi taberna preferida.*

  2. Me gusta hablar español. _____

  3. Mi hermano toca el tamvor. _____

  4. Es un toro muy vrabo. _____

  5. Mis amigos me regalan un móbil nuevo. _____

2. Choose the correct word in the sentences below.

  1. Mi plato favorito es el ~~poyo~~ / *pollo* frito.

  2. El haya / halla es un árbol.

  3. La vaca / baca da leche.

  4. El niño halla / haya su puesto.

  5. Los barcos navegan hacia la boya / bolla roja.

3. Complete the following words with the correct letter, 'll' or 'y'.

  1. *ll*ave (key)

  2. bo____o (bun)

  3. a____er (yesterday)

  4. ____over (to rain)

  5. ____ ate (yacht)

4. Complete the words below with the correct letter, 'b' or 'v'.

  1. *b*e*b*er (to drink)

  2. ____illa (town)

  3. ____elleza (beauty)

  4. ca____ello (hair)

  5. ____er____o (verb)

14

LET'S MAKE FUNNY NOISES
SOME LETTERS AND THEIR SOUNDS

- **C / K / Q / Z.** 'K' and 'q' are always pronounced as the 'k' in 'kinks', and 'z' is always pronounced as the 'th' in 'thinks'. 'C' is pronounced like 'k' and 'q' when it appears before 'a', 'o' and 'u', and it is pronounced like 'z' before 'e', 'i' or a consonant. 'Q' is always followed by a mute 'u' and either 'e' or 'i'.

  > *casa* (house) – *cosa* (thing) – *acusar* (to accuse)
  >
  > *cena* (supper) – *cine* (cinema)
  >
  > *clara* (light) – *cristal (glass)* – *cruel* (cruel)
  >
  > *queso* (cheese) – *paquete* (packet) – *quinto* (fifth) – *maqueta* (model)

  'K' is, like 'w', a very rare letter in Spanish. It mainly appears at the beginning of the word. With the exception of words starting with *kilo-*, words with 'k' are of clear foreign origin.

  > *kiwi* (kiwi)   *keniata* (Kenyan)
  >
  > *kibutz* (kibbutz)   *kayak* (kayak)

  Due to the similar pronunciation, several spellings are acceptable for some words with this sound.

  > *klaxon /claxon* (klaxon)
  >
  > *kiosco /quiosco* (kiosk)
  >
  > *kimono /quimono* (kimono)

- **G / J.** 'J' is always pronounced like a strong English 'h'. 'G' is pronounced exactly the same before 'e' and 'i' (as in *género* [gender] and *gitano* [gypsy]). Otherwise, it is pronounced like English 'g' in words like **g**ángster (**g**angster) and **g**araje (**g**arage). [In this last orthographic point the letters and sequences in bold show a similar pronunciation in both languages.]

  If the letter 'u' is included between the 'g' and the 'e' or between the 'g' and the 'i', it is also pronounced like English 'g' and the 'u' is mute.

  > *guerra* (war)   *guinda* (morello cherry)
  >
  > *gueto* (ghetto)   *guitarra* (guitar)

  In both cases the 'u' is pronounced if it has an umlaut, which is indicated by two little dots on top: 'ü'.

  > *vergüenza* (shame)   *güisqui* (whisky)   *lingüística* (linguistics)

5. Correct 'k', 'c', and 'z' in the following sentences if necessary.

1. Me duele la kabeza. ➟ *Me duele la cabeza.*

2. María estudia química en la universidad. _____

3. Estamos en la cozina. _____

4. En verano comemos zerezas. _____

5. Me encantan las hamburguesas kon quetchup. _____

6. Choose the correct word in the sentences below.

1. Comemos bocadillos de ~~gamón~~ / *jamón*.

2. Vamos a tocar la guitarra / gitarra.

3. Dame un vaso de ajua / agua.

4. No tengo relog / reloj.

5. El pájaro / págaro canta en el campo.

7. Match the words that have the same initial sound.

1. guerra   a) cuero

2. casa   b) gato

3. cero   c) jardín

4. gente   d) zapato

8. Complete the words below with the correct letter, 'g' or 'j'.

1. gelatina (jelly)

2. ___i___ante (giant)

3. ___abón (soap)

4. ___ue___o (game)

5. ___irafa (giraffe)

15 THIS ONE OR THAT ONE?
DEMONSTRATIVE DETERMINERS AND PRONOUNS

- 'This', 'that', and their respectively plurals, 'these' and 'those', are used to refer to something that is known by the speaker, specifying its proximity to him and the listener, either in a physical or figurative sense. In English we only have two forms with their corresponding plurals, but in Spanish we have three and we have to distinguish not only between singular and plural, but also between masculine and feminine.

- *Este* and *esta* and their corresponding plurals, *estos* and *estas*, like 'this' and 'these', refer to something that is close to the speaker.

este (masc. sing.)	*estos* (masc. plur.)
esta (fem. sing.)	*estas* (fem. plur.)

- 'That' can be translated by *ese* or *aquel* (and their respective related forms: *esa* or *aquella*); in the same way, 'those' can be translated by *esos* and *aquellos* (also with their respective related forms: *esas* or *aquellas*).

- *Ese* is used for something either relatively distant from both speaker and listener, or closer to the listener than to the speaker; *aquel* is used for something similarly far or remote from both.

ese (masc. sing.)	*esos* (masc. plur.)
esa (fem. sing.)	*esas* (fem. plur.)
aquel (masc. sing.)	*aquellos* (masc. plur.)
aquella (fem. sing.)	*aquellas* (fem. plur.)

- A similar distinction is made for *aquí* (here) and *ahí, allí/allá* (there). *Ahí* is closer to the speaker than *allí/allá*.

1. Connect each phrase in Spanish to its best equivalent in English.

1. Este traje   a) These chairs

2. Esa manzana   b) Those trees

3. Aquel río   c) This suit

4. Estas sillas   d) That river

5. Aquellos árboles   e) That apple

2. Put each demonstrative in brackets in the correct form.

1. (aquel) *Aquellos* camiones.

2. (ese) _____ televisiones.

3. (este) _____ caballo.

4. (aquel) _____ vaca.

5. (ese) _____ calle.

3. Make grammatical phrases selecting a word from each of the three columns below.

1. Esa	cuadros	rota	*Esa mesa rota.*
2. Aquella	vela	veloces	_____
3. Estas	balón	hermosos	_____
4. Estos	aves	larga	_____
5. Ese	mesa	redondo	_____

4. Translate the following sequences into Spanish.

1. This exam. ➡ *Este examen.*

2. Those fast trains (over there). _____

3. That weird place (near you). _____

4. Those girls. _____

5. That little lioness. _____

15 · THIS ONE OR THAT ONE?
DEMONSTRATIVE DETERMINERS AND PRONOUNS

- Demonstratives take the gender and number of the noun they precede:

  este libro interesante
  (this interesting book)

  ese niño listo
  (this clever child)

  aquel coche grande
  (that big car)

  esta historia triste
  (this sad story)

  esa señora buena
  (that kind lady)

  aquella playa tranquila
  (that peaceful beach)

  estos hospitales nuevos
  (these new hospitals)

  esos zapatos viejos
  (those old shoes)

  aquellos niños pequeños
  (those small children)

  estas casas rojas
  (these red houses)

  esas faldas cortas
  (those short skirts)

  aquellas bebidas frías
  (those cold drinks)

- Demonstratives can occasionally appear after the noun if it is preceded by a definite article. This is a colloquial and slightly emphatic use for referring to something in a physical or figurative sense.

  El caso *ese* es famoso (That case is well known).

- If the demonstrative is not followed by a noun, it takes the gender and number of the noun it replaces and is written with an accent on the first 'e' from the left:

  éste blanco
  (this white one)

  ése morado
  (that purple one)

  aquél beige
  (that beige one)

  ésta amarilla
  (this yellow one)

  ésa azul
  (that blue one)

  aquélla gris
  (that gray one)

  éstos naranjas
  (these orange ones)

  ésos verdes
  (those green ones)

  aquéllos marrones
  (those brown ones)

  éstas rosas
  (these pink ones)

  ésas rojas
  (those red ones)

  aquéllas negras
  (those black ones)

- Furthermore, there are three neuter singular forms which refer to an event or something indeterminate or collective: *esto* (this), *eso* (that which is near you or relatively distant from both) and *aquello* (that which is far over there). Note that they are not written with an accent because they cannot be mistaken for any other form.

  No entiendo **esto** (I don't understand this).

  Eso *pasa siempre* (That always happens).

  ¿Qué es **aquello**? (What is that over there?).

5. Complete the sentences below with the correct word from the box.

> este – esa – aquel – estas – aquellos

1. Me gusta *esa* camisa.
2. Podemos sentarnos en _____ bancos.
3. _____ rosas son mis favoritas.
4. Tenemos que tomar _____ autobús.
5. _____ coche es de mi padre.

6. Make whatever corrections are necessary in the following sentences.

1. Aquéllas rosas son hermosos. ➡ *Aquellas rosas son hermosas.*
2. Ese ordenador es potente. _____
3. Éstos juguetes son muy bonitos. _____
4. Aquel es fuerte. _____
5. Ésto no me gusta. _____

7. Put the accent on the demonstrative in the phrases below when necessary.

1. Aquellos. ➡ *Aquéllos.*
2. Este pequeño. _____
3. Esas radios. _____
4. Aquellas tazas blancas. _____
5. Eso maravilloso. _____

8. Complete with *este / estos / esta /estas / esto* with or without an accent.

1. *Éstos* son nuestros hijos.
2. _____ libro es muy largo.
3. _____ no lo entiendo.
4. _____ toallas están mojadas.
5. Esa libreta es tuya, _____ es la mía.

16 YOUR TURN OR MY TURN?
POSSESSIVE DETERMINERS AND PRONOUNS

- The possessives take different forms depending on the possessor (I, you, he/she/it, we, you, they), the number of items possessed (one or more) and, in two cases, the gender of the item(s) possessed.

POSSESSOR	THE ENTITY POSSESSED		
	SINGULAR	PLURAL	
	MASC. FEM.	MASC. FEM.	
I	mi	mis	(my)
You (informal)	tu	tus	(your)
You (formal)	su	sus	(your)
He/She/It/They	su	sus	(his/her/its/their)
We	nuestro nuestra	nuestros nuestras	(our)
You	vuestro vuestra	vuestros vuestras	(your)

- Note that *su* and *sus* are also used for 'your', corresponding to the formal *usted* or *ustedes*.

  Mis *problemas* (my problems).   **Nuestras** *escuelas* (our schools).

  Tu *coche* (your car).   **Sus** *chistes* (his/her/their/your jokes).

  Usted no se preocupe, **su** *dinero está seguro en* **nuestro** *banco* (Don't worry, your money is safe in our bank).

- The identity of the possessor in *sus chistes* above can only be disambiguated in a larger, more informative context.

1. Complete the sentences below with the correct word from the box.

mi – tu – su – nuestros

1. Sonia y Felipe lavan *su* coche.
2. Nosotros hacemos _____ deberes.
3. María da de comer a _____ gato.
4. Yo quiero mucho a _____ hermano.
5. Tú siempre llegas tarde a _____ trabajo.

2. Fill in the gaps with the corresponding possessor.

1. **Mi** abrigo (yo).
2. _____ corbata (ellos).
3. _____ bufandas (él).
4. _____ guantes (tú).
5. _____ pantalones (vosotras).

3. Translate the following sentences.

1. This is my spoon. ➡ *Ésta es mi cuchara.*
2. They are her records and tapes. _____
3. This is his blue lorry. _____
4. They sell our vases and your frames. _____
5. The cat lives in your house. _____

4. Make whatever corrections you find necessary:

1. Son mías amigas. ➡ *Son mis amigas. / Son amigas mías.*
2. Estos personas son mi madre y padre. _____
3. Suyas flores. _____
4. Mis profesoras. _____
5. Tus balón y muñeca. _____

16

YOUR TURN OR MY TURN?
POSSESSIVE DETERMINERS AND PRONOUNS

- If the possessed item is not present, the possessives change. These possessives are also used after the noun with a slightly emphatic effect.

    Los **suyos** quieren más (Theirs want more).

    El coche **nuestro** da muchos problemas (Our car gives a lot of problems).

POSSESSOR	THE ENTITY POSSESSED				
	SINGULAR		PLURAL		
	MASC.	FEM.	MASC.	FEM.	
I	mío	mía	míos	mías	(mine)
You (informal)	tuyo	tuya	tuyos	tuyas	(yours)
You (formal)	suyo	suya	suyos	suyas	(yours)
He/She/It/They	suyo	suya	suyos	suyas	(his/hers/its/theirs)
We	nuestro	nuestra	nuestros	nuestras	(ours)
You	vuestro	vuestra	vuestros	vuestras	(yours)

- Note that, as with the other possessives, *suyo, suyos, suya* and *suyas* are also used for formal 'your'.

    Este lápiz es **suyo**, no lo deje ahí.
    (This pen is yours, don't leave it there.)

- In order to disambiguate *su* and its related forms, we can use *de + él /ella / ellos /ellas /usted /ustedes*.

    Aquellos alumnos son (los) **suyos** /de ellos.
    (Those pupils are his / hers / theirs.)

    Son **suyos** /Son de ellos.
    (They are his / her / theirs.)

- This type of possessive may appear in different positions with respect to the verb.

    Este bolígrafo es (el) **mío** (This pen is mine).

    Es **mío** (It is mine).

    La **tuya** tiene cuatro habitaciones (Yours has four rooms).

    Es la **tuya** (It is yours).

The articles in brackets are optional and emphatic.

5. Choose the correct option in the sentences below.

1. Esta granja es ~~tu~~ / *tuya*.

2. Mi / mío bolso es nuevo.

3. Ellos se quedan en nuestra / nuestro casa.

4. Ellos comen en su / suya terraza.

5. Vuestro / vuestra almacén es muy grande.

6. Create correct sentences using the information in brackets about the possessor.

1. Estos vestidos son *míos* (yo).

2. Ésta es la _____ (tú).

3. Aquella letra es _____ (ellas).

4. Eso es _____ (ella).

5. Nuestra casa es la _____ (vosotros).

7. Rephrase the following sentences by adding a suitable possessive.

1. Esta flor es mía. Es *mi* flor.

2. Ése es mi novio. Es _____.

3. Aquellas ovejas son de María. Son _____.

4. La cocina es tuya. Es _____ cocina.

5. El pez es de Juan y José. Es _____ pez.

8. Write the correct order to make sentences.

1. diccionario / el / mío / es ➡ *El diccionario es mío.*

2. bicicleta / esa / de / es / ellas _____

3. tu / tengo / dirección _____

4. nuestra / casa / es / ésta _____

5. coche / vuestro / aquí / está _____

17 I AM STUDYING THIS LESSON
THE GERUND AND THE PRESENT PROGRESSIVE

- The verbs in the progressive form are used to indicate actions in progress (e.g., *Estoy corriendo tan rápido como puedo,* 'I am running as fast as I can'), and formed with the verb *estar* (to be) followed by the main verb ending in *-ando* or *-iendo* (gerund or -ing form), depending on whether it is the first conjugation or any of the two others.

-AR	-ER	-IR
caminar (to walk)	*correr* (to run)	*escribir* (to write)
estoy caminando	estoy corriendo	estoy escribiendo
estás caminando	estás corriendo	estás escribiendo
está caminando	está corriendo	está escribiendo
estamos caminando	estamos corriendo	estamos escribiendo
estáis caminando	estáis corriendo	estáis escribiendo
están caminando	están corriendo	están escribiendo

- Like the rest of verbal endings, these forms may be irregular:

  leyendo (reading; from leer)   *cayendo* (falling; from *caer*)
  yendo (going; from *ir*)   *trayendo* (bringing; from *traer*)
  huyendo (escaping; from *huir*)   *oyendo* (hearing; from *oír*)
  viniendo (coming; from *venir*)   *viendo* (seeing; from *ver*)
  pidiendo (asking for; from *pedir*)   *diciendo* (saying; from *decir*)
  mintiendo (lying; from *mentir*)   *sintiendo* (feeling; from *sentir*)

- In Spanish there are no restrictions as to the type of verb that can be used in this form.

  Estoy viendo a Mary al final de la calle (I can see Mary at the end of the road / *I am seeing Mary at the end of the road).

1. Provide the gerund of the following verbs. Firstly, try to form it by applying the standard rule and then, secondly, check it in case it has an irregular gerund.

1. Esperar ➡ *esperando*

2. Atender _____

3. Asentir _____

4. Pagar _____

5. Inventar _____

6. Vender _____

7. Descubrir _____

8. Comprar _____

9. Participar _____

10. Negar _____

2. Put the simple present verbs in brackets in the present continuous.

1. *Estoy comprobando* (compruebo) los resultados.

2. _____ (juegas) con tus amigos.

3. _____ (ojea) una revista.

4. _____ (sentimos) frío.

5. _____ (encendéis) el ordenador.

3. Match the words in the two columns to make complete sentences.

1. Yo

2. El niño

3. Los pájaros

4. El sol

5. Hoy

a) están cantando

b) está lloviendo

c) está jugando

d) estoy estudiando

e) está brillando

4. Correct the following sentences if necessary.

1. Raquel está deciendo la verdad. ➡ *Raquel está diciendo la verdad.*

2. Estoy leyendo un libro de aventuras. _____

3. Los presos están huiendo de la cárcel. _____

4. El mendigo está pediendo una limosna. _____

5. Mi padre está escuchendo la radio. _____

17

I AM STUDYING THIS LESSON
THE GERUND AND THE PRESENT PROGRESSIVE

- Progressive verbs are used less in Spanish than in English. In Spanish they tend to imply greater duration or repetition of the verbal action.

  Brief action:

  Whom are you talking to? ⮕ *¿Con quién* **hablas**? (simple present).

  Spontaneous speech:

  What are you doing? ⮕ *¿Qué* **haces**? (simple present).

  Immediate future:

  I'm coming back tonight. ⮕ **Vuelvo** *esta noche* (simple present).

- An -ing form in English may correspond to an infinitive in Spanish:

  With a verb that expresses likes or dislikes:

  I hate swimming in cold water. ⮕ *Odio* **nadar** *en agua fría*.

  With some prepositions:

  The sportsman prays after training and before running. ⮕ *El deportista reza después de* **entrenar** *y antes de* **correr**.

  Acting as a noun:

  Sleeping is my favourite hobby. ⮕ **Dormir** *es mi hobby favorito* (in this case, the infinitive can be preceded by an optional *el*).

- Conversely, a gerund in Spanish may not correspond to an -ing form in English:

  Time (to indicate two parallel actions):

  Estando *en España hablo español.* ⮕ When/While I am in Spain, I speak Spanish.

  Cause (to indicate a major circumstance):

  Siendo *presidenta tiene más responsabilidades.* ⮕ Since she is a president she has more responsibilities.

  Manner (to indicate the way in which the action takes place):

  Entra **corriendo**. ⮕ He runs inside (literally: 'He enters running').

5. In the following sentences, decide if the English gerund corresponds to the Spanish infinitive or gerund and add the equivalent verb form.

1. My sister loves swimming. Infinitive — *nadar*.

2. I'm buying a pair of shoes. _____

3. Running every morning is very healthy. _____

4. She always knocks before opening the door. _____

5. They are opening the windows. _____

6. Fill out the gaps with a simple present or a present continuous verb according to the message.

1. *Vuelvo* (yo / volver) a las siete para cenar.

2. _____ (tú / hacer) un ejercicio de español.

3. _____ (alguien [somebody] / llamar) a la puerta.

4. _____ (nosotros / esperar) el autobús.

5. _____ (ellas / ir) a la cama a las diez y media todos los días.

7. Cross out the verb that does not correspond in each sentence.

1. El público lanza claveles al cantante después de *aplaudir* / *aplaudiendo*.

2. Ir / Yendo al parque libero las tensiones del trabajo.

3. Los niños salen del colegio saltar / saltando.

4. Detestan dormir / durmiendo en el suelo.

5. Reír y llorar / Riendo y llorando son acciones saludables.

8. Translate the following sentences into Spanish.

1. You arrive waving your hands. ➧ *Llegas saludando con las manos.*

2. As we are the owners, we are responsible for (de) the mess.

_____

3. I do my homework on my way / as I go to school.

_____

4. They wash the plates after eating.

_____

5. I love playing with your puppy.

_____

18 NEVER SAY *NUNCA MÁS*

NEGATIVE SENTENCES AND NEGATION WORDS

- Negating an action in Spanish is very simple: ***no*** (no, not) is put before the verb.

    No *quiero más patatas, gracias* (I don't want more potatoes, thank you).

    No *duermo durante el día* (I don't sleep during the day).

    No *soy alemán, soy sueco* (I am not German, I'm Swedish).

- There are several other negation words that can be used instead of *no*: *nadie* (no one, nobody), *nada* (nothing), *nunca* (never), *jamás* (never) and *ningún / ninguno /ninguna /ningunos /ningunas* (none).

    Nadie *es perfecto* (Nobody is perfect).

    Nada *me asusta* (Nothing frightens me).

    Nunca *salimos* (We never go out).

    Jamás *llora* (He never cries).

    Ninguno *de los libros me gusta* (I don't like any of the books / I like none of the books).

- When the negated element appears after the verb, ***no*** stays.

    No *veo a* ***nadie*** *de mi familia* (I don't see anybody from my family / I see nobody from my family).

    Margaret ***no*** *pide* ***nada*** *más* (Margaret doesn't ask for anything else / Margaret asks for nothing else).

    No *conducen* ***nunca*** *por Madrid* (They never drive in Madrid).

    No *queremos* ***ningún*** *problema* (We don't want any problems).

1. Rewrite the following sentences in the negative form.

1. Son las ocho menos cuarto. ➡ *No son las ocho menos cuarto.*

2. Arreglo tu vestido largo. _____

3. Estamos estudiando español. _____

4. Estas modistas cosen la ropa. _____

5. Los juguetes están en la caja. _____

2. Rewrite the following sentences in the affirmative form.

1. No quiero ir al colegio. ➡ *Quiero ir al colegio.*

2. Parece que no va a llover esta mañana. _____

3. Nunca tiene dinero. _____

4. A María no le apetece comer ensalada hoy. _____

5. No lee ningún folleto. _____

3. Rephrase the following sentences starting with the word *no*.

1. Jamás vemos a tu tía Maribel. ➡ *No vemos jamás a tu tía Maribel.*

2. Nadie quiere problemas en vacaciones. _____

3. Nunca sabemos la lección de historia. _____

4. Nada tiene sentido. _____

5. Nadie teme a Virginia Woolf. _____

4. Order the following fragments to make correct sentences.

1. Con amigos / no / nunca / salimos ➡ *No salimos nunca con amigos.*

2. Al payaso listo / nadie / nunca / aplaude _____

3. De la historia / nadie / nada / cree _____

4. Jamás / a una discoteca / no / vamos _____

5. Quiero / muñeca / ninguna / no _____

18

NEVER SAY *NUNCA MÁS*
NEGATIVE SENTENCES AND NEGATION WORDS

- Negations *ni* and *ni … ni* are used for negating two or more similar items in a sentence.

    Jamás* / *Ni van al cine *ni* salen a comer por ahí (They never/don't go to the cinema or eat out).

    No* / *Ni estudian *ni* trabajan (They neither study nor work).

- *No … ni* is incorrect when subjects are involved.

    Ni Pedro *ni* Luisa trabajan (Neither Peter nor Mary work).

- *Ni* can be used in front of each item in a list for emphatic purposes.

    Mis amigos **no** estudian **(ni)** francés, **(ni)** inglés, **ni** italiano (My friends don't study French, English or Italian).

- Unlike in English, it is possible to combine more than one word of negation in the sentence.

    No viajo ***nunca*** con ***nadie*** / ***Nunca*** viajo con ***nadie*** (I never travel with anybody).

    No dice ***nadie nada*** / ***Nadie*** dice ***nada*** (Nobody says anything).

- *Nunca* can be emphasized by appending *jamás* (never ever) or *más* (never again). Other negations are emphasized by adding *en absoluto* (at all) at the end of the sentence. Informally, adjectives can also be preceded by *nada* (at all) and *jamás* followed by *en la vida* ('in my / your /… life').

    Nunca jamás miramos al pasado / ***No*** miramos nunca jamás al pasado (We never ever look at the past).

    Nunca más hablaré con ella / ***No*** hablaré nunca más con ella (I won't talk to her ever again).

    No me gusta este coche **en absoluto** (I don't like this car at all).

    No estás **nada** guapa con ese vestido (You really don't look nice in that dress).

    No volverá ***jamás en la vida*** (He/She will never come back again in his/her life).

5. Complete the sentences with the correct word from the box.

nunca – jamás – ni – nadie – nada

1. **Nada** es como antes.
2. No come _____ carne _____ pescado.
3. No quiere ver a _____.
4. Mi primo _____ estudia para los exámenes.
5. Ella _____ usa pantalón.

6. Emphasize the following negations.

1. El barco no va hacia tierra. ➠ *El barco no va nunca/jamás hacia tierra.*
2. No vamos al museo de cera.

   _____

3. Después de esta experiencia, no comemos ostras en julio.

   _____

4. Aquellos niños no juegan con el balón.

   _____

5. Pedro no fotografía animales, edificios ni vehículos.

   _____

7. Correct the following sentences if necessary.

1. No el hipopótamo ni la jirafa son carnívoros.

   ➠ *Ni el hipopótamo ni la jirafa son carnívoros.*

2. Después del accidente, más jamás cruzamos el río en barca.

   _____

3. No en absoluto suspende ninguna asignatura. _____
4. Esto no es nada razonable. _____
5. Él nunca sabe ni la hora, ni el día, el mes. _____

8. Translate the following sentences into Spanish.

1. He doesn't have any friends at all. ➠ *No tiene ningún amigo en absoluto.*
2. I'm not going anywhere with you! _____
3. My daughter never gets up late. _____
4. I will never go back to my country. _____
5. There isn't anything in the cupboard. _____

19

MAY I ASK YOU A QUESTION?

INTERROGATIVE AND EXCLAMATIVE SENTENCES

- In Spanish questions and exclamations have both an opening and a closing sign: '¿ ?' and '¡ !'. Like in English, there cannot be a full stop immediately after a closing sign.

    ¿Qué pasa? (What is the matter?).

    ¡Silencio! (Silence!).

- The subject and verb positions in questions may or may not be inverted. Obviously, this option is not available when there is no explicit subject.

    ¿Tú vas al cine esta noche? (Are you going to the cinema tonight?)

    ¿Vas tú al cine esta noche? (Are you going to the cinema tonight?)

    Son de Granada (They are from Granada).

    ¿Son de Granada? (Are they from Granada?)

- These are called 'yes-no questions'. In Spanish, the answers to these questions typically oscillate between one word and a whole sentence. The short answer type 'yes, we are' or 'no, we aren't' is not normally used in Spanish.

    ¿Estáis casados? Sí (Are you married? Yes).

    ¿Estáis casados? Sí, estamos casados (Are you married? Yes, we are married).

    *¿Estáis casados? *Sí, estamos* (Are you married? Yes, we are).

1. Put these sentences in the interrogative form.

1. Los niños juegan en el jardín. ➠ *¿Juegan los niños en el jardín?*

2. La tarta es de chocolate. _____

3. El cartero odia a los perros. _____

4. La película es fascinante. _____

5. A Antonio le gustan los helados. _____

2. Match the questions and the answers.

1. ¿Te gusta el fútbol?   a) No, no practican ningún deporte.

2. ¿Tienen hambre?   b) Sí, gracias. Hace mucho calor.

3. ¿Eres española?   c) No, acaban de desayunar.

4. ¿Juegan al tenis?   d) Sí, me gusta ver los partidos en el estadio.

5. ¿Queréis beber algo fresco?   e) No, soy portuguesa.

3. Make questions for the following answers.

1. *¿Está tumbado en el sofá?* Sí, está tumbado en el sofá.

2. ¿_____? No, tengo un televisor.

3. ¿_____? No, leo esa revista.

4. ¿_____? Sí, escriben guiones de cine.

5. ¿_____? No, no funciona la lavadora.

4. Order the following words to make correct interrogative sentences (add the question marks).

1. Raquel / ropa / compra / mucha

   ➠ *¿Compra Raquel mucha ropa?*

2. los / son / niños /de / todos / Madrid

   _____

3. corredores / muy / están / los / cansados

   _____

4. manzana / gusta / tarta / te / de / la

   _____

5. al / tarde / por / cine / la / ellos / van

   _____

19 MAY I ASK YOU A QUESTION?
INTERROGATIVE AND EXCLAMATIVE SENTENCES

- In order to ask for a precise piece of information, questions start with certain key words and the order of the rest of the words remains intact. Note the accents that differentiate them from the equivalents used in statements.

  ¿Qué? (What) ➡ *¿Qué hora es?* (What time is it?)

  ¿Cuándo? (When) ➡ *¿Cuándo vas al museo?* (When do you go to the museum?)

  ¿Dónde? (Where) ➡ *¿Dónde están mis llaves?* (Where are my keys?)

  ¿Cómo? (How) ➡ *¿Cómo estás?* (How are you?)

  ¿Por qué? (Why) ➡ *¿Por qué no descansas?* (Why don't you rest?)

- Some of these words can change according to gender and/or number: *cuál / cuáles, quién /quiénes, cuánto /cuánta /cuántos /cuántas.*

  ¿Quién? (Who) ➡ *¿Quiénes quieren más?* (Who wants more?)

  ¿Cuál? (Which) ➡ *¿Cuál es tu comida favorita?* (Which is your favourite food?)

  ¿Cuánto? (How much/many) ➡ *¿Cuántas vacas ves?* (How many cows can you see?)

- These words can be preceded or followed by others to elicit different types of information (when this word is a preposition it always goes at the beginning of the question).

  ¿A qué hora *llega el tren?* (What time does the train arrive?)

  ¿Con quién *vienes?* (Who are you coming with?)

- Exclamations may be formed by simply adding the corresponding marks at both ends of any sentence. Alternatively, characteristics may be emphasized by putting *qué* at the front of the exclamation. In these constructions, subject / verb inversion is not possible with personal pronouns other than *usted* and *ustedes*. Otherwise, it is.

  ¡Brasil gana el campeonato! *¡Qué Brasil gana el campeonato!* (Brazil has won the championship!)

  ¡La niña es preciosa! *¡**Qué** preciosa (es la niña)!* (What a beautiful girl!; how beautiful!)

  ¡Conduce veloz! *¡**Qué** veloz (conduce)!* (How fast [he drives]!)

  ¡Eres tú un genio! *¡Tú eres un genio!* *¡Es usted un genio!* *¡Usted es un genio!* (You are a genious!)

  *¡**Qué** hombre más/tan guapo!* (What a handsome man!)

5. Add ¡ ! or ¿ ? to these sentences.

1. Qué día tan agradable ➠ *¡Qué día tan agradable!*

2. Dónde vive tu padre _____

3. Eres una gran amiga _____

4. Por qué no vienes al cine _____

5. Eres ruso o ucraniano _____

6. Make questions for the following answers.

1. *¿Cuál es tu coche?* Es el rojo.

2. ¿_____? Porque hay mucho atasco en la carretera.

3. ¿_____? Viven en Paris.

4. ¿_____? Tiene veintitrés.

5. ¿_____? Me gustan las de terror.

7. Translate the following questions and exclamations.

1. Who does my baby love: daddy or mummy?

   ¿A quién quiere mi niño, a papá o a mamá?

2. Since when do they brush their teeth alone?

   _____

3. How long have you been working for?

   _____

4. Where do you come from?

   _____

5. This music is marvellous!

   _____

6. What beautiful buildings!

   _____

8. Answer the following questions.

1. ¿Cuántos hijos tienes? _____

2. ¿Hasta dónde cabalgas los jueves? _____

3. ¿Cuánto pagas por el menú en ese bar? _____

4. ¿Hacia dónde van aquellas ovejas? _____

5. ¿Cuánto cuestan esos pendientes? _____

20 MISS, MRS. OR MS., MADAM?
WAYS OF ADDRESSING PEOPLE

TUTÉEME.

- As we have already mentioned in unit 4, **usted** is a polite form which shows respect. Remember also that although *usted*, like the Spanish *tú* and the English 'you', refers to the listener, the verb endings and possessives are the same as those used with the third person singular subject. Hence, in order to avoid ambiguities, it is possible to say *de usted* instead of *su, suyos* or their respective related forms.

  Usted es *el siguiente* (You are the next one).

  Tiene *que esperar* **usted** *media hora* (You have to wait for half an hour).

  La habitación **de usted** *es aquélla* (Your room is that one over there).

- There is also a formal equivalent of *vosotros/as* in the plural: **ustedes**. Similarly, the verb endings and the possessives are the same as the ones used for the third person plural.

  ¿Cómo **cocináis** *la paella?* (How do you [colloquial] cook paella?)

  ¿Cómo **cocinan (ustedes)** *la paella?* (How do you [formal] cook paella?)

- In Spanish it is less common than in English to use personal titles such as Mr., Mrs., etc. The equivalents are **señor** and **don** (and their related forms); both are only used to address somebody you treat as *usted*.

- **Don** and **doña** are used in singular and with the first name (optionally followed by the surname). They have no plural.

  Don *Sebastián* (Mr. Sebastian).   **Doña** *Pilar Martínez* (Ms. Pilar Martínez).

  Doña *Cristina está en la puerta* (Ms. Christina is at the door).

1. In the sentences, decide if the construction is formal or informal.

1. Vosotros tenéis que quedaros aquí. ➠ Iɴꜰᴏʀᴍᴀʟ.

2. Entre usted el primero. _____

3. ¿Qué desean ustedes para cenar? _____

4. Tú vienes conmigo al cine. _____

5. Señora, ha llegado su marido a recogerla. _____

2. Put a suitable title in front of the following names.

1. **Don** Ricardo García.

2. _____ Mónica.

3. _____ Hortensia Pérez.

4. _____ Carlos.

5. _____ Cándido Varela Méndez.

3. Make corrections where necessary.

1. Ustedes no soléis ir a las cuatro menos veinte.

➠ **Ustedes no suelen / Vosotros no soléis ir a las cuatro menos veinte.**

2. Aquellas historias son de tú. _____

3. Éstas son sus plantas, son suya. _____

4. ¿Cómo ustedes van a la universidad diariamente? _____

5. ¡Es usted muy (very) amable! _____

4. Fill out the gaps in the following sentences about the formal second person.

1. **Usted** es muy amable, gracias.

2. Vd. _____ las plantas semanalmente.

3. No es mi abrigo, es el _____.

4. Son _____ documentos, no los míos.

5. _____ están en _____ casa.

20

MISS, MRS. OR MS., MADAM?
WAYS OF ADDRESSING PEOPLE

- *Señor, señores, señora* and *señoras* are used before the surname (optionally preceded by the first name) in a formal and/or professional context.

    Señorita and *señoritas* are reserved for young ladies and can be used with the first name or the surname. With all these titles the definite article is used for indirect reference.

    > *Señor García, pase por favor* (Mr. García, come in please).

    > *La señorita Julia Jurado al teléfono* (Ms. Julia Jurado on the phone).

- *Señores* followed by *de* and the surname can be used to refer to a married couple but it is considered rather formal. A similar expression to the English 'the Freemans' is also used in Spanish, but the surname is not in plural:

    > *Los señores de Rodríguez Pérez* (Mr. and Mrs. Rodríguez Pérez).

    > *Los Fernández llegan mañana* (The Fernández arrive tomorrow).

- Spanish women do not lose their maiden surnames when they get married.

- On envelopes in formal correspondence both titles can be found together and abbreviated:

    > *Sr. D. Federico Alba* (Mr. Federico Alba)

    > *Sra. D.ª Lucía Varela* (Mrs. Lucia Varela)

- In Spain *vos* is really an archaism, which comes from the contraction of the expression *Vuestra Merced* ('Your Worship'), in this case a respectful expression used with monarchs, the Pope, etc. The verb is used in the second person plural. In Latin America, however, *vos* is used very informally as the second person singular, with the verb in the singular too, and in Argentina it is the standard form.

    > *Vos, Majestad, sois muy amable* (Your Majesty is very kind).

    > *Vos estás muy contenta hoy* (You are very happy today).

- In Latin America in general the only second plural form is *ustedes*.

5. Match the following fragments to build full titles; think of the different possibilities.

1. La señora   a) Martínez
2. Los   b) Juan Mora
3. La señorita   c) Rodríguez
4. Sr. D.   d) Cristina Losada
5. Los señores de   e) Ana

6. Fill out the sentences below with the adequate word.

1. Los *señores* de Álvarez Ruiz no vendrán a la fiesta.
2. El _____ Hernández no podrá atenderle hoy.
3. La _____ Belén está ocupada en este momento.
4. _____, su ilustrísima, tenéis razón como siempre.
5. Esta carta viene a la atención de _____ Rubén Prado.

7. Translate the following sentences into Spanish.

1. How big your (plural formal) car is! ➡ *¡Qué grande es su coche!*
2. How do you (singular formal) prefer your meat: rare, medium or well done?
   _____
3. Those records are yours (singular informal).
   _____
4. Your (plural informal) mice are eating the lettuce.
   _____
5. Are you (plural formal) happy with your lives?
   _____

8. Order the following words to make correct sentences.

1. señores / García / los / son / de / simpáticos ➡ *Los señores de García son simpáticos.*
2. una / ustedes / hora / terminar / para / tienen
   _____
3. Juan / llega / don / mañana
   _____
4. es / Julio / carta / González / la / Sr. / para / D. / el
   _____
5. tienen / nuevo / los / apartamento / Pérez / un
   _____

21 Diagnosis: stress

Marking accented syllables

- Like in English, all words in Spanish have one syllable (whatever is pronounced all at once; it can be a vowel or a group of letters) that is pronounced slightly longer and at a higher pitch than the rest.

  con**trol** (first syllable counting from the right)

  refrige**ra**tor (second)

  marvellous (third)

- Except for the obvious case of words consisting of only one syllable (e.g., *pez* [fish], *luz* [light]), it is very hard to know where the accented syllable will be without having heard the word first. Having said that, the majority of Spanish words with two and even three syllables have their accent on the second syllable from the right, particularly if they end in a vowel, 'n', or 's'. Long words often have the accent placed on the third syllable from the right.

ac**triz** (actress)	**plan**ta (plant)	espec**tá**culo (show)
ca**jón** (drawer)	**mo**to (moped)	te**lé**fono (telephone)
vu**dú** (voodoo)	**ca**ja (box)	fan**tás**tico (fantastic)
es**quí** (ski)	di**fí**cil (difficult)	**plás**tico (plastic)

- As you can see from the examples above, sometimes the vowel of the accented syllable receives a written accent '´'. All types of words (nouns, adjectives, etc.) may receive a written accent. In Spanish vowels may receive signs of two types: '´' and '¨' (see unit 14).

- The rules for marking an accented syllable when writing are very simple. Some indicate a deviation from the general pronunciation norm stated above (therefore, they never apply to words with one syllable); others distinguish between identical words (mainly grammatical words [articles, prepositions, etc.] and verbs; see unit 15).

1. All of these words need a written accent. Add them in.

1. Sofa   *Sofá*
2. Melon   _____
3. Arbol   _____
4. Esplendido   _____
5. Romantico   _____

2. One of these words does not need a written accent. Which one?

1. Ramón   _____
2. Judía   _____
3. Ferrocarríl   _____
4. Bebé   _____
5. Práctico   _____

3. Which is the correct word of the two options given?

1. Está estudiando ~~ingles~~ / inglés.
2. Me robo / robó mi cartera.
3. El canto / cantó de los pájaros me despierta.
4. Son las cuatro y media / medía.
5. Te espero en el anden / andén (platform).

4. Correct the following sentences if necessary.

1. Mi portatil está estropeado, dejame el tuyo.

➡ **Mi portátil está estropeado, déjame el tuyo.**

2. El avion llego con retráso al aeropuerto.

_____

3. La guia de telefonos es muy útil.

_____

4. La exposicion fué un éxito.

_____

5. El delfín víve feliz en el oceano.

_____

21

DIAGNOSIS: STRESS
MARKING ACCENTED SYLLABLES

- A word that finishes in a vowel, 'n' or 's' and whose most prominent syllable is the first one from the right receives a written accent.

ciem**piés** (centipede)	pa**ís** (country)	israe**lí** (Israeli)
bu**ró** (bureau)	ca**fé** (coffee)	Cor**fú** (the island)
lec**ción** (lesson)	car**mín** (rouge)	ra**tón** (mouse)

- Conversely, a word that finishes in a consonant other than 'n' or 's' and whose most prominent syllable is the second from the right receives a written accent.

por**tá**til (portable)	**ár**bol (tree)	**lá**piz (pencil)
a**zú**car (sugar)	ca**dá**ver (corpse)	**fá**cil (easy)
hábil (skilful)	**crá**ter (crater)	**fér**til (fertile)

- All words whose most prominent syllable is neither the first nor the second one, receive a written accent too.

éxito (success)	mag**ní**ficamente (magnificently) [see unit 26]
para**plé**jico (paraplegic)	**fá**brica (factory)
sar**có**fago (sarcophagus)	pris**má**ticos (binoculars)
ta**rán**tula (tarántula)	hi**pó**dromo (racetrack)

- Rules regarding accents are compulsory, even with capital letters, and may distinguish between words.

  PANADERÍA PÉREZ / Panadería Plácido Pérez (Pérez Bakery)

  mana (it flows) – *maná* (manna)

  ingles (groins) – *inglés* (English)

  carne (meat) – *carné* (identification card)

- In the following identical pairs, one takes a written accent and the other does not.

WITHOUT A WRITTEN ACCENT	WITH A WRITTEN ACCENT
el (the)	*él* (he)
o (or, when it appears between words)	*ó* (or, when it appears between figures)
mi (my)	*mí* (me)
tu (your)	*tú* (you)
si (if)	*sí* (yes; himself/herself/themselves)
se (himself/herself/themselves)	*sé* (I know; be!)
de (of)	*dé* (he may/should give)
aun (even)	*aún* (still/yet)
mas (but)	*más* (more/most/plus)
solo (alone)	*sólo* (only)
te (you, to/for you)	*té* (tea)

5. Write all the accents needed in the sentences below.

1. Lleva un telefono movil. ➡ *Lleva un teléfono móvil.*

2. Esta leyendo el periodico. _____

3. Todos tomamos cafe con azucar. _____

4. Las plantas estan sin regar. _____

5. Veo muchas peliculas en aleman. _____

6. Choose the correct word of each pair.

1. Si / Sí no vienes, yo no voy.

2. Tiene tres o / ó cuatro coches.

3. ¿Quien / Quién juega?

4. ¡Que / Qué día tan hermoso!

5. No te quedes solo / sólo en este bosque.

7. Complete the following sentences with the correct word: *el/él, tu/tú*.

1. El ordenador de *tu* padre no funciona.

2. _____ no me gusta nada; ella sí.

3. _____ tienes que venir con _____ amiga.

4. _____ casa es más bonita que la de _____.

5. _____ jardín de mi abuela es enorme.

8. Translate the following sentences into Spanish.

1. Ramon's truck is at the station. ➡ *El camión de Ramón está en la estación.*

2. The birds build their nest on the trees.

_____

3. The doctor is at the clinic.

_____

4. Your photograph album has fantastic landscapes.

_____

5. We are going on a trip to the botanical gardens.

_____

22 ECONOMIZING
OBJECT PERSONAL PRONOUNS

- Just as the identity of the subject (the agent or doer of the action of a sentence, e.g., 'Manhattan', 'my upstairs neighbour') can be substituted by a brief personal pronoun (e.g., 'it', 'he'), other parts of the sentence can be abbreviated as well by substituting them for other pronouns.

- When the direct object (see unit 2) is substituted by a pronoun, it does not appear behind the conjugated verb like the equivalent full forms, but right before it.

> I admire Susan. ➡ *Admiro a Susan.*
> I admire her. ➡ ***La** admiro.*
>
> I lend a book. ➡ *Presto un libro.*
> I lend it. ➡ ***Lo** presto.*
>
> You draw the fruits. ➡ *Pintáis las frutas.*
> You draw them. ➡ ***Las** pintáis.*

me ➡ *me*	us ➡ *nos*
you ➡ *te*	you ➡ *os*
him / it (masc. animate) ➡ *lo / le*	them (masc. animate) ➡ *los / les*
him / it (masc. inanimate) ➡ *lo*	them (masc. inanimate) ➡ *los*
her / it (fem. animate) ➡ *la / le*	them (fem. animate) ➡ *las / les*
her / it (fem. inanimate) ➡ *la*	them (masc. inanimate) ➡ *los*

- As can be seen, for the third person it must be considered whether the entity is a human being or a high order animal.

1. Rephrase the following sentences using suitable personal pronouns instead of the underlined fragments.

1. Mónica come la manzana. ➠ *Mónica la come.*

2. Los niños tiran la pelota. _____

3. Mi madre compra un bolso. _____

4. Los pintores pintan las paredes. _____

5. Sergio paga los regalos. _____

2. Complete the sentences below with a suitable pronoun.

1. **Me** pruebas la camisa (You try the shirt on me).

2. _____ quitas los documentos (You take the documents away from her).

3. _____ abres la puerta del tren (You open the train door for them).

4. _____ lavas la ropa (You wash the clothes for us).

5. _____ mandas un paquete (You send me a parcel. / You send a parcel to me).

3. Complete the sentences below with a personal pronoun from the box using the information in brackets as a clue.

| la lo las los |

1. María **los** pide a su madre (unos favores).

2. Nosotros _____ arreglamos gratis (las averías).

3. Ellos _____ pagan en dólares (la compra).

4. Tú _____ ofreces (una ayuda).

5. El humo _____ advierte (la existencia de un incendio).

4. Translate the following sentences.

1. My father speaks to me in Chinese. ➠ *Mi padre me habla en chino.*

2. I invite you to the cinema. _____

3. They call her insistently. _____

4. You open it abruptly. _____

5. The grandfather looks at them. _____

- Remember that the formal second person (*usted* and *ustedes*) takes the same pronouns as the third person (see unit 20).

  Yo **la/le** escucho (I listen to you).

  Yo **los/les** espero (I wait for you).

- When the recipient (see unit 2) is substituted by a pronoun, it also appears before the verb. The only pronoun that is different from the ones seen so far is the third one.

him / her / it ➡ **le**	them ➡ **les**

  He offers lottery to his friends. ➡ *Ofrece lotería a sus amigos.*

  He offers lottery to them. ➡ ***Les** ofrece lotería.*

- If both types of pronoun coincide in the sentence, the indirect object (recipient) pronoun precedes the direct one, and it is **se** for the third person both singular and plural.

  We decorate the room for you. ➡ *Decoramos la habitación para ti.*

  We decorate it for you. ➡ ***Te la** decoramos.*

  She buys a present for her mother. ➡ *Compra un regalo a su madre.*

  She buys it for her. ➡ ***Se lo** compra.*

- With commands, infinitives and gerunds, both direct and indirect pronouns are appended to the verb form (see unit 27).

  *¡Cóme**telo** todo!* (Eat everything up!)

  *Hay que limpiar**lo** (el suelo).* (It – the floor – has to be cleaned.)

  *Estoy terminándo**la** (la novela).* (I'm finishing it – the novel.)

5. Rephrase the following sentences using suitable personal pronouns instead of the underlined fragments.

1. Manuel vende <u>mantas a mi madre</u>. ➡ *Manuel se las vende.*

2. La cocinera prepara <u>la tarta a los novios</u>. _____

3. Maite pinta <u>cuadros al rey</u>. _____

4. La costurera cose <u>trajes a los actores</u>. _____

5. Preparo <u>juegos para los estudiantes</u>. _____

6. Make grammatical sentences by selecting fragments from both columns.

1. Me lo ⟍   a) ruego encarecidamente.

2. Se te ⟍ ➡   b) dices ahora.

3. Te las   c) colocan ellos en la solapa.

4. Os lo   d) ve en la cara.

5. Nos los   e) devuelven intactos.

7. Correct the position and choice of the personal pronouns in the sentences below.

1. Les yo limpio la alfombra. ➡ *Yo les limpio la alfombra.*

2. Ellos arreglan les los juguetes. _____

3. Vosotros contestáis nos las preguntas. _____

4. Las lámparas os alumbran. _____

5. Dan las les fotografías. _____

8. Choose the appropriate form taking into account the information in brackets.

1. Las / Los hago con mi madre (los deberes).

2. Les / las presté un libro (a mis amigas).

3. Las / los escribimos todos los días (las cartas).

4. No quiero verles / verlas (las películas).

5. Tenemos que comerlos / comerlas (los bocadillos).

23 ECONOMY REVISITED

PERSONAL PRONOUNS WITH PREPOSITIONS

- If you want to briefly refer to something after a preposition, you can use one of the pronouns below:

1st singular: *mí*	1st plural: *nosotros*
2nd singular: *ti*	2nd plural: *vosotros*
3rd singular: *él / ella / ello*	3rd plural: *ellos / ellas*

*Trabajan **para mí*** (They work for me).

*Voy **detrás de ti*** (I go after you).

*No estoy segura **de ello*** (I am not sure about it).

*Ellos vienen **con nosotras*** (They come with us).

*Hoy como **sin vosotros*** (I eat without you today).

*Estamos **delante de ellos*** (We are in front of them).

- Note the written accents in the first and third persons for distinguishing purposes (see unit 21).

   *Ese lugar es para **mí*** (That place is for me).

   ***Mi** regalo es muy frágil* (My present is very fragile).

1. Match words from the two columns to create a correct and plausible sentence.

1. Ellos corren   a) con él.
2. Elena viaja   b) la fiesta sin ti.
3. Oscar no confía   c) una mesa para vosotros.
4. El carpintero construye   d) detrás de nosotros.
5. No podemos empezar   e) en mí.

2. Translate the following sentences into Spanish.

1. We walk in front of you. ⟹ *Nosotros caminamos delante de ti/vosotros/usted/ustedes.*
2. You go out with them. _____
3. They collect it for us. _____
4. He does it for you. _____
5. You promise it to me. _____

3. Correct the following sentences if necessary.

1. Tu nombre me se olvida siempre. ⟹ *Tu nombre siempre se me olvida.*
2. Compro les un libro por su cumpleaños. _____
3. Encontré en el jardín la. _____
4. Te ayudo en tu trabajo. _____
5. Me invitan a ti a la fiesta. _____

4. Choose the correct form of the two provided paying attention to the accent.

1. Mi / mí salón es grande. ⟹ *Mi salón es grande.*
2. El / él reloj está parado. _____
3. No sabe vivir sin mi / mí. _____
4. Lo compré para el / él. _____
5. El / él chico no recibe mucha ayuda. _____

ECONOMY REVISITED
PERSONAL PRONOUNS WITH PREPOSITIONS

- As an exception, the preposition **con** (with) forms one word with the first and second person singular pronouns.

1st singular: **conmigo**	1st plural: **con nosotros**
2nd singular: **contigo**	2nd plural: **con vosotros**
3rd singular: con **él / ella / ello**	3rd plural: **con ellos / ellas**

Como **contigo** *hoy* (I eat with you today).

Vamos de excursion **con vosotros** (We go on an excursion with you).

Colaboramos **con ellas** (We collaborate with them).

- It is extremely common to duplicate the information of the objects, that is, to state the full object together with the corresponding pronoun that goes before the verb.

Le *compra el jersey* **a su madre** (He buys the jumper for his mother).

Se *lo compra* **a su madre** (He buys it for his mother).

Esa película la *vi ayer* (I saw that film yesterday).

- In the case of the 1st and 2nd persons, adding the prepositional phrase is optional and emphatic.

Me *lo deben* **a mí** (They owe it to me).

A mí *no* **me** *cuentes historias* (Don't tell me stories).

A nosotros *no* **nos** *respetan* (They don't respect us).

5. Join each sentence in Spanish with its equivalent in English.

1. Él corre conmigo todas las mañanas.   a) They bring me cakes.
2. Me traen pasteles.   b) She/He cooks it for her every morning.
3. Se lo cocina (a ella) todas las mañanas.   c) She goes shopping with you.
4. A ella no la quieren.   d) He runs with me every morning.
5. Ella va contigo de compras.   e) They don't love her.

6. Fill in the gaps below with phrases starting with *con* and *sin*, and using the clue provided in brackets.

1. Salimos *contigo* (tú).   Salimos *sin ti* (tú).
2. Vienen _____ (yo).   Vienen _____ (yo).
3. Acaban _____ (ellas).   Acaban _____ (ellas).
4. Estudiáis _____ (nosotros). Estudiáis _____ (nosotros).
5. Paseo _____ (él).   Paseo _____ (él).

7. Add a pronoun to the following sentences to obtain a duplicating and/or emphatic effect.

1. *Se* lo pido a mis amigos.
2. _____ las venden a mí a bajo precio.
3. _____ la compramos a nuestros amigos.
4. _____ la venden a vosotras.
5. _____ les escapan las cometas.

8. Rephrase the following sentences using suitable personal pronouns instead of the underlined fragments.

1. Mis amigos pasean al lado de las chicas. ➠ *Ellos pasean al lado de ellas.*
2. Mis hermanas no conocen a mi novia. ➠ _____
3. Los ciudadanos comprenden a su presidente. ➠ _____
4. La madre lleva la bolsa sin asa. ➠ _____
5. Mi marido baila con su mujer. ➠ _____

24 EXCUSE ME, PLEASE... THANK YOU!
POLITE EXPRESSIONS

- It must be said that it is not so common in Spanish to use formulae of politeness in every single communicative situation as it is in English, particularly in informal contexts. Politeness is conveyed by a kind tone of voice or by using questions rather than orders (often with a form of the verb *poder*; see unit 27 for the formation of orders).

  ¿Me enseña sus papeles? /¿Le importaría enseñarme sus papeles? (Could you show me your papers?)

  ¿Podría guardar silencio? /¿Sería usted tan amable de guardar silencio? (Could you be quiet?)

- You can use these expressions if you want to, and you will certainly create a good impression, but do not get upset or make any wrong assumptions if people do not use them with you!

- As seen in unit 12, the typical polite word used to ask for permission is *por favor* (please). The position of polite words in the sentence is rather free, like in English.

  *Sus documentos, **por favor*** (Your documents, please).

  ***Por favor,** guarde silencio* (Please, be quiet).

- Gratitude is generally expressed with the word *gracias* (thanks). It can be emphasized by adding *muchas* or *muchísimas*. You can make a sentence stating the reason for your gratitude; in that case the preposition that follows *gracias* is *por* followed by an infinitive verb.

  ***Muchas gracias,** es usted muy amable* (Thank you very much, you are very kind).

  ***Gracias** por participar en el debate* (Thank you for participating in the discussion).

- The typical polite reply to somebody who says *gracias* is *de nada*, but you may also hear *a ti* or *a usted* (thank **you**).

1. Choose the correct expresion: *por favor* or *gracias*.

1. La documentación del coche, **por favor**.
2. _____ por todas sus atenciones.
3. _____ , no debe moverse.
4. _____ , no fume aquí.
5. _____ , tiene mucha paciencia.

2. Transform these sentences using the word or words in brackets.

1. ¡Siéntate! (por favor). ➡ *¡Siéntate, por favor!*
2. Me ha gustado mucho la comida (muchas gracias).

   _____

3. ¿Le abres la puerta? (ser tan amable).

   _____

4. ¿Puedes esperarme un momento? (importar).

   _____

5. Ayúdame con las bolsas (poder).

   _____

3. Transform these orders into polite questions without using *por favor*.

1. Abra la maleta. ➡ *¿Podría / Le importaría abrir la maleta?*
2. Cierra la ventana. _____
3. Ponte de pie. _____
4. Hazme una taza de café. _____
5. Déjeme pasar. _____

4. Order the following words to make correct sentences.

1. gracias / comprarme / muchas / por / regalo / este.
   ➡ *Muchas gracias por comprarme este regalo.*
2. abrir / importaría / les / puerta / la.

   _____

3. el / empiecen / por / examen / favor.

   _____

4. ayudarme / la / preparar / comida / gracias / a / por.

   _____

5. Tan / apagar / amable / luz / sería / de / la.

   _____

24 EXCUSE ME, PLEASE... THANK YOU!
POLITE EXPRESSIONS

- Apologies can be given with the noun *perdón* (sorry) or the verb *perdonar* (to forgive). Again, you can make a full statement by using the preposition *por* followed by an infinitive verb. The person to be forgiven is introduced by **a** or with an object pronoun (see previous units 22 and 23).

  Perdón, *es culpa mía* (Sorry, it's my fault: this is an idiomatic expression).

  Perdone a *mi hijo* **por** *ser tan directo* (Forgive my child for being so direct).

  Perdóname por *olvidar tu cumpleaños* (Forgive me for forgetting your birthday).

- *Perdón*, *perdona*, etc. are also used in the situations where in English you use 'excuse me': to call somebody's attention, to let somebody know he/she is in the way, etc.

  Perdone, *¿puede decirme qué hora es?* (Excuse me, could you tell me what time it is?)

  Perdón, *¿puedo pasar?* (Excuse me, can I come in?)

- Another common way to express apologies is by means of the verb *sentir* (to be sorry). You can either produce a short version with *lo* before the verb, or a full expression with an infinitive verb (and no preposition).

  Lo siento (I'm sorry).

  Lo siento **mucho** (I'm very sorry).

  *¡**Cuánto** lo siento!* (I'm so sorry!).

  Siento molestarles (Sorry to bother you).

- Polite replies to somebody who apologises include *no es nada, no se preocupe, no te preocupes,* and *no tiene importancia.*

  Sentimos *despertarte a las dos de la mañana* (We are sorry to wake you up at two in the morning).

  No tiene importancia, *enseguida vuelvo a dormirme* (It doesn't matter, I'll go back to sleep immediately).

5. Chose the most suitable option for each sentence.

1. ~~Gracias~~ / *Perdónale* por romper el jarrón.

2. Perdón / Muchas gracias por todos los regalos.

3. Cuánto perdón / siento la muerte de tu hermano.

4. ¿Me ayudas a estudiar la lección, gracias / por favor?

5. Perdón / gracias, ¿puede decirme donde está la estación?

6. Translate the following sentences into Spanish.

1. Thank you very much for your kind words. ➡ *Muchas gracias por tus amables palabras.*

2. I am sorry for arriving without the shopping. _____

3. Please, give me a break. _____

4. I apologise for its terrible condition. _____

5. You are welcome; it's a pleasure. _____

7. What would you say in the following circumstances?

1. You step on someone's toes. ➡ *Perdón. / Lo siento (mucho). / ¡Cuánto lo siento!*

2. You want to call the shop assistant's attention. _____

3. You are very late for your date. _____

4. You have just been given a nice / horrible present. _____

5. You have not quite understood what the other person said. _____

8. Make whatever corrections are necessary to the following polite sentences.

1. ¿Les da, por favor, las llaves? _____

2. Sentimos por causar problemas a su familia. _____

3. Gracias por soportar cuatro horas de ensayo. _____

4. No tienen importancia. _____

5. Perdona mi vecina molestar a esta hora de la noche. _____

Bond, James Bond

Introductions and farewells

- The following are common
  expressions in personal
  introductions. Note that the three
  sequences below have a similar
  meaning but are increasingly more
  informal.

  *Hola, ¿cómo está? Me llamo Juan
  López, ¿cuál es su nombre?*
  (Hello, how are you? My name is
  Juan López, what is your name?)

  *Hola, ¿qué tal? Me llamo Juan
  López, ¿y usted?*
  (Hello, how are you? My name is
  Juan López, and yours?)

  Hola, ¿qué hay? Soy Juan López, ¿y tú?
  (Hello, how is it going? I'm Juan López, and you?)

- If a third person is doing the introduction, there is a standard construction,
  which varies slightly according to the relative status of the persons being
  introduced (see unit 20 for the different titles).

  *Sr. Martínez, permítame presentarle a Tomás Rodríguez.
  Tomás, el Sr. Martínez.*

  (Mr. Martínez, may I introduce you to Tomás Rodríguez.
  Tomás, this is Mr. Martínez).

  Juan, te presento a Lola. Lola, éste es Juan.
  (Juan, let me introduce you to Lola. Lola, this is Juan).

- There are also different replies according to the level of formality which you
  wish to convey. The following sequences are increasingly more informal.

  Sr. Martínez: Tanto gusto (How do you do?)
  Tomás: El gusto es mío (How do you do?)

  Sr. Martínez: Encantado (How do you do?)
  Tomás: Igualmente (How do you do?)

  Sr. Martínez: ¿Qué tal? (How are you?)
  Tomás: Bien, gracias, ¿y tú? (Fine, thanks, and you?)

1. In the following sentences, decide if the construction is formal or informal.

1. Hola, ¿cómo estáis? ➡ INFORMAL

2. Le presento al Sr. López. _____

3. ¿Cómo te llamas? _____

4. María, ésta es Carmen. _____

5. Encantada de conocerle. _____

2. Provide a reply to the following comments.

1. ¿Cómo estás? ➡ *Muy bien, gracias. ¿Y tú?*

2. Ha sido un placer conocerle. _____

3. Encantada. _____

4. Éstos son los Sres. de Madera. _____

5. ¿Cuál es su nombre, por favor? _____

3. Make corrections to the sentences below if necessary.

1. Tantos gustos. ➡ *Tanto gusto.*

2. ¿Qué es su nombre? _____

3. Me llaman Pablo Fuentes. _____

4. El gusto es mi. _____

5. Encantada de conocerle. _____

4. Match the questions and the answers. Pay attention to the level of formality.

1. Hola, ¿qué tal?   a) Mónica, ¿y tú?

2. ¿Cómo está usted?   b) Mi nombre es Blanca Pérez

3. ¿Cómo te llamas?   c) Fenomenal, gracias

4. ¿Cómo se llama usted?   d) Muy bien, ¿y usted?

5. ¿Cómo te va?   e) Bien, ¿y tú?

- The most common way to greet somebody is by saying *hola* (hello). This can be substituted or followed by another greeting specific to a part of the day (see unit 37).

    Hola, buenos días (Good morning).

    Buenas tardes (Good afternoon/evening).

    Adiós, buenas noches (Good night). [See below.]

- Below are some fragments of dialogue that can be heard when two people are talking for the first time. Note that the main differences between English and Spanish have been highlighted.

    – *¿**De dónde** es usted?* (Where are you from?)

    – *Soy originalmente de Bilbao, pero vivo en Madrid.* (I'm originally from Bilbao, but I live in Madrid).

    – *¿**Cuánto tiempo lleva** en Madrid?* (How long have you been in Madrid?)

    – ***Unos** seis años* (Six years, more or less).

    – *¿**A qué se dedica**?* (What do you do for a living?)

    – *Soy profesora de español* (I'm **a** Spanish teacher).

    – *¿Dónde trabaja?* (Where do you work?)

    – *En una academia de idiomas* (In a language school).

    – *¿Tiene una tarjeta profesional **aquí**?* (Do you have a business card with you?)

    – *No, no **llevo** ninguna* (No, I haven't got one on me).

    – *¿**Me da** su teléfono o su email, por favor?* (Can I have your telephone number or your email, please?)

    – *Sí, desde luego (*Yes, of course).

- When saying goodbye a different formula is used.

    *Ha sido un placer, adiós (*Pleased to meet you, goodbye).

    Lo mismo digo (Same to you).

- The word to say goodbye in Spanish varies according to whether and when you expect to see the other person next:

    Adiós (Goodbye).   *Hasta pronto* (See you soon).

    Hasta luego (See you later).   *Hasta ahora* (See you in a few minutes).

- There is also the possibility of stating a fixed time using *hasta* and the time:

    Hasta mañana (See you tomorrow).

    Hasta la semana que viene (See you next week).

    Hasta dentro de una hora (See you in an hour).

5. Match the questions and the answers.

1. ¿De dónde es usted?

2. ¿Me dan su tarjeta, por favor?

3. ¿Hace mucho que vive usted en Barcelona?

4. ¿Me da su dirección, por favor?

5. ¿Qué hace usted?

a) Por supuesto: calle Rosalía de Castro, 56.

b) Me dedico a las ventas.

c) He nacido en Sevilla, pero vivo en Córdoba.

d) Lo sentimos, pero no tenemos ninguna aquí.

e) No mucho, tres meses.

6. Find suitable questions for the following answers.

1. *¿A qué te dedicas? / ¿Qué haces?* – Estudio.

2. ¿_____? – En la Universidad de Málaga.

3. ¿_____? – Farmacia.

4. ¿_____? – En tercero.

5. ¿_____? – Lo siento, no tengo conexión
   a Internet todavía.

7. Fill in the following gaps if necessary.

1. *Le* presento al Sr. Director.

2. ¿_____ dónde trabaja?

3. ¿_____ qué se dedica?

4. ¿_____ tal está?

5. ¿_____ tiene una tarjeta?

8. Translate the following sentences into Spanish.

1. Can I have your address, please? ➡ *¿Me da su dirección, por favor?*

2. What is your name? _____

3. My name is Susana Martín. _____

4. Same to you. _____

5. How do you do? _____

- In order to qualify actions and states we use words like 'slowly', 'often', 'there', etc. We can classify them into four groups, according to the type of information they provide: place, time, quantity and manner.

- Place adverbs contribute with spatial content and tend to appear at the end of the sentence.

  *La siguiente gasolinera está **lejos**, no **cerca*** (The next petrol station is far from here, not nearby).

  *¿Vives **allí**? No, **aquí*** (Do you live [over] there? No, here).

- The information about time can either say when something happens (a point in time) or how often something happens (a frequency pattern).

  *Sara llega de París **mañana*** (Sarah arrives from Paris tomorrow).

  *El curso termina **en Navidad*** (The course ends at Christmas).

  ***Siempre** voy al colegio en autobús, aunque **a veces** voy en coche con mi padre, pero **nunca** voy en taxi* (I always go to school by bus, although sometimes I go by car with my dad, but I never go by taxi).

- The adverbs which provide information about quantity are normally placed after the verb, with the exception of *casi* (almost) and *apenas* (hardly), which are placed before.

  *Mi hija come **demasiado*** (My daughter eats too much).

  ***Apenas** tengo tiempo para descansar* (I hardly have any time to rest).

1. Decide if the following adverbs express time, place or quantity.

   1. Abajo ➡ PLACE.

   2. Ahora ➡ _____

   3. Entonces ➡ _____

   4. Bastante ➡ _____

   5. Arriba ➡ _____

2. Select time words from the table to complete the sentences below.

a menudo – raramente – nunca – siempre – a veces

   1. No te veo *nunca*.

   2. Nos visitamos _____.

   3. _____ ordeno la habitación.

   4. Nos escribimos _____ por Navidad.

   5. Voy al cine _____.

3. Select plausible place words to complete these sentences (do not repeat them).

ahí – aquí – enfrente – lejos – cerca

   1. Te veo *enfrente*.

   2. ¿Estás _____?

   3. Atropelló a un motorista _____, en este punto.

   4. Viven muy _____, a más de 1.000 km (more than 1,000 km away).

   5. Nuestras casas están _____, sólo se tarda cinco minutos en llegar.

4. Use these adverbs to express quantity or extent.

casi – poco – mucho – apenas – nada

   1. *Casi* atropello a un motorista.

   2. Falta _____ para terminar (We are close to finishing).

   3. _____ tenemos tiempo.

   4. Ellos tienen _____ dinero, son millonarios.

   5. La bolsa no tiene _____, está vacía.

- The information about the manner in which an action takes place is typically provided by words like *rápidamente* (quickly), *cariñosamente* (lovingly), *agresivamente* (aggressively), etc. As can be seen, they are formed from a feminine singular adjective, *rápida, cariñosa, agresiva,* plus the ending *-mente* (usually corresponding to the English -ly ending). Note that adverbs take the written accent in exactly the same way as the adjective from which they are formed (e.g., *tímidamente, ágilmente*).

- However, the formation process described above is not always possible (e.g., **amarillamente, *pequeñamente*). Two well know exceptions are *bien* (well) and *mal* (wrongly, badly).

- The words ending in *-mente* are usually long, so they tend to occur at the end of the sentence, unless there are other longer complements in the sentence or you want to give them special emphasis (see unit 2 for the general rules of word order in the sentence).

  *Conduce **cuidadosamente*** (He drives carefully).

  *Canta **suavemente** a los niños de su clase* (He sings gently to the children in his class).

- Sometimes the word qualifying the action has the form of the masculine singular adjective, but this is not frequent.

  *Esa pluma escribe **fino** /*finamente* (That fountain pen writes finely).

  *Habla muy **bajo** /*bajamente* (He speaks quietly).

  *¿Come **mucho** o **poco**?* (Does he/she eat much or little?)

- In other occasions both forms are possible.

  Ven rápidamente (norm) */Ven rápido* (exception) (Come quickly).

  Trabajan duramente /Trabajan duro (They work hard).

- If two or more of these regularly formed words come together, *-mente* only appears in the last one.

  *Trabajamos **intensa** y **metódicamente*** (We work intensely and methodically).

  *¿Lo hacemos **discreta** o **abiertamente**?* (Shall we do it discreetly or openly?)

5. Form adverbs ending in _-mente_ out of the following adjectives when possible.

    1. Lento ⟹ _lentamente._

    2. Blanco ⟹ _____

    3. Claro ⟹ _____

    4. Difícil ⟹ _____

    5. Intrínseco ⟹ _____

6. Use these adverbs to express manner.

> amablemente – rápidamente – duro – lentamente – atropelladamente

    1. María cruzó la calle **rápidamente.**

    2. Entraron _____ en la habitación.

    3. Todos en la familia me trataron muy _____.

    4. La enfermera le puso la inyección muy _____.

    5. Los jugadores entrenan _____ toda la semana.

7. Complete the sentences below with suitable adverbs ending in _-mente_ equivalent to the words in brackets.

    1. Cosen las cortinas **cuidadosamente** (with care).

    2. Viene _____ (with haste).

    3. Esperas _____ (with impatience).

    4. Se mueven _____ (very slowly).

    5. Charlan _____ (in a friendly way).

8. Correct the following sentences if necessary.

    1. Levanta las piedras lentamente y pesadamente.

    ⟹ **Levanta las piedras lenta y pesadamente.**

    2. Esta máquina funciona buenamente. _____

    3. Estas joyas se venden baratamente. _____

    4. Trabajan duro. _____

    5. Termino este ejercicio felizmente. _____

27 STAND AT EASE!
POSITIVE AND NEGATIVE COMMANDS

- Direct commands ('come!', 'go!')
  are always given to a 2nd person
  (the interlocutor). This can be
  singular or plural, formal or
  informal. The form of the
  command depends on the
  conjugation (see unit 3).

	-AR	-ER	-IR
SINGULAR INFORMAL	habla	vende	divide
SINGULAR FORMAL	hable	venda	divida
PLURAL INFORMAL	hablad	vended	dividid
PLURAL FORMAL	hablen	vendan	dividan

- The subject is not necessary, but it can appear emphatically. In this case, it
  usually follows the verb, although it may precede it if the speaker wants to call
  the attention of his/her interlocutor(s) when they are in a large group. It is,
  therefore, appropriate in environments like a classroom or military
  headquarters.

  Seguid vosotros (You carry on).

  Paguen ustedes en caja (Pay at the checkout).

  ¡Usted, *cállese!* (Be quiet, you!)

  ¡Tú, *sal* a la pizarra! (You, go to the blackboard!)

1. Make commands from the following verbs for the persons in brackets.
   Then translate the command into English.
   1. Continuar (informal singular) ⟹ *Continúa (Go on).*
   2. Ceder (informal plural) ⟹ _____
   3. Competir (formal singular) ⟹ _____
   4. Estirar (formal plural) ⟹ _____
   5. Encoger (formal singular) ⟹ _____

2. Decide if these commands are formal or informal.
   1. Corre. ⟹ *INFORMAL.*
   2. Ande. ⟹ _____
   3. Salga. ⟹ _____
   4. Juega. ⟹ _____
   5. Viaje. ⟹ _____

3. Add a suitable subject pronoun to the following commands.
   1. _____, ven aquí por favor. ⟹ *Tú, ven aquí, por favor.*
   2. Cabalguen deprisa _____. ⟹ _____
   3. Barred _____. ⟹ _____
   4. ¡_____, contemplen esto! ⟹ _____
   5. Apostad _____ por esta yegua. ⟹ _____

4. Order the following sentences (remember you are giving commands).
   1. esa / ventana / abran. ⟹ *Abran esa ventana.*
   2. silla / comprad / esa. _____
   3. ahí / chaqueta / ponga / esta. _____
   4. el / televisor / enciende. _____
   5. acaba / todo / café / el. _____

27

STAND AT EASE!
POSITIVE AND NEGATIVE COMMANDS

- Remember that you can incorporate *por favor* into your command to soften it and make it more polite (see unit 24).

    ¡Levántese, por favor! (Stand up, please).

    ¡Venid aquí inmediatamente, por favor! (Come here immediately, please).

    Por favor, termina ya el ejercicio (Please finish the exercise).

    Baja, por favor, el volumen (Please lower the volume).

- Negative commands vary for both informal forms. Note that the second and third conjugations are identical.

	-AR	-ER	-IR
SINGULAR INFORMAL	no habl**es**	no vend**as**	no divid**as**
PLURAL INFORMAL	no habl**éis**	no vend**áis**	no divid**áis**

   *No **cante** usted tan alto, por favor* (Please, do not sing so loudly).

   *No **cambiéis** el ritmo de la música ahora* (Don't change the rhythm of the music now).

   *No **alquiles** una furgoneta tan vieja* (Don't hire such an old van).

- Another use of commands corresponds to the English expression 'let's'. The Spanish equivalent uses the first person plural of the verb:

    ***Vamos** /**Vayamos** todos* (Let's go all of us).

    ***Acabemos** de una vez por todas* (Let's finish once and for all).

5. Make corrections wherever necessary.

1. Dejan los abrigos en el armario, por favor. ➠ *Dejen los abrigos en el armario, por favor.*

2. Encended la luz ustedes, por favor. _____

3. Tome tú esta maleta tan pesada. _____

4. Usted, crea un nuevo estilo de prenda para este invierno.

   _____

5. Crea en mis palabras, te lo aseguro. _____

6. Put the following commands in the negative form.

1. Para. ➠ *No pares.*

2. Reconsidere. ➠ _____

3. Plantead. ➠ _____

4. Vuelen. ➠ _____

5. Vuelvan. ➠ _____

7. Make correct commands by linking sentence fragments from each of the two columns.

1. Por favor,   a) tengas miedo.

2. Tú no   b) lo olviden.

3. Vosotros no   c) escucha esta noticia.

4. No   d) traiga el postre.

5. Ustedes, no   e) estéis nerviosos.

8. Translate the following sentences into Spanish.

1. Leave that box there (formal plural). ➠ *Dejen esa caja allí.*

2. Finish your homework (informal singular). ➠ _____

3. Stop making that noise (informal plural). ➠ _____

4. Don't open this door (informal plural). ➠ _____

5. Use the yellow towel (formal singular). ➠ _____

28 ONCE UPON A TIME...

SIMPLE PAST TENSES

¡ LO OLVIDÉ !

- There are two ways to express the past tense in Spanish, apart from the historical use of the present tense seen in unit 10. One of them alludes to the duration of actions, without indication of their beginning or end (it is often used for actions which either were long in time [such as 'lived'], or took place in a repeated or regular way [e.g., 'went to work every day']). The endings are as follows.

	-AR	-ER	-IR
Yo	escuch**aba**	perd**ía**	viv**ía**
Tú	escuch**abas**	perd**ías**	viv**ías**
Él/Ella	escuch**aba**	perd**ía**	viv**ía**
Nosotros	escuch**ábamos**	perd**íamos**	viv**íamos**
Vosotros	escuch**abais**	perd**íais**	viv**íais**
Ellos	escuch**aban**	perd**ían**	viv**ían**

- Note that the endings for the second and third conjugations are identical.

- In English this tense can be translated by using the simple past, and also by the continuous 'was/were -ing', 'used to' and even 'would'.

    *¿Qué **hacías**?* (What were you doing?)

    *Durante los primeros años **iba** al colegio con mis padres* (During the first years I went / used to go / would go to school with my parents.)

1. Fill out the sentences below with the correct word from the box.

salíais – cantábamos – corrían – tomabas – coleccionaba

1. Tú **tomabas** siempre la galleta más grande.
2. _____ la misma canción en clase todas las mañanas.
3. _____ de paseo todas las tardes en verano.
4. Arturo _____ cromos de jugadores de fútbol.
5. Mis vecinos _____ por la calle.

2. Provide the most suitable verb of the following three: *saludar, jugar* and *vivir* in the past for each context.

1. En 1984 **vivía** en esta casa con mis padres.
2. Durante mi infancia _____ al fútbol los domingos con los niños de mi barrio.
3. Cuando _____ en Manchester _____ con el Manchester United.
4. Aquel maquinista siempre _____ a la gente con la mano.
5. Pedro _____ en Paris cuando tenía diez años.

3. Translate the following sentences into Spanish.

1. The clock struck (dar) twelve and everybody clapped.

   ➠ *El reloj daba las doce y todo el mundo aplaudía.*

2. After parties, people used to phone the host to thank (para agradecer) the invitation.

   _____

3. In autumn the gardeners would prune the trees for the rest of the year.

   _____

4. When (cuando) it was raining the children stayed at home.

   _____

5. When I was little I had a beautiful Chinese doll.

   _____

4. Put the infinitives in brackets in the correct past form.

1. Ella (tirar) **tiraba** las cajas a la basura por la noche.
2. La pareja (preparar) _____ la cena para los invitados.
3. Los niños se peleaban y luego (volver) _____ a jugar.
4. El padre (trabajar) _____ en el despacho hasta el anochecer.
5. La familia siempre (felicitar) _____ a la abuela en su cumpleaños.

28

ONCE UPON A TIME...
SIMPLE PAST TENSES

- The other way to express the past presents the verbal action as already completed and it corresponds to a particular moment in time. It is generally used for shorter actions (like 'jumped', 'sighed').

  *Mi madre nació **en 1927*** (My mother was born in 1927).

  *Juan terminó el libro **ayer*** (John finished the book yesterday).

- This tense can only be translated by the simple past in English ('-ed' in the case of regular verbs).

	-AR	-ER	-IR
Yo	salt**é**	corr**í**	sal**í**
Tú	salt**aste**	corr**iste**	sal**iste**
Él/Ella	salt**ó**	corr**ió**	sal**ió**
Nosotros	salt**amos**	corr**imos**	sal**imos**
Vosotros	salt**asteis**	corr**isteis**	sal**isteis**
Ellos	salt**aron**	corr**ieron**	sal**ieron**

- Note again that the second and third conjugations take the same endings.

- Note also that the first person plural in the first and third conjugations is identical to that of the simple present. However, the communicative context is likely to prevent any ambiguity.

  Jugamos *a la pelota hasta que nos **llamó** mi madre* (We played with the ball until our mum called us).

- Since it is common for the second person singular to finish in the letter **s** in other verb tenses, there is a common mistake which consists of adding an **s** to the ending of the past, like **saltastes*.

  Llegaste *a las dos en punto* (You arrived at two o'clock).

5. Conjugate both types of past tense for the following infinitives:
lograr, comer, partir.

lograba	logré	comía	comí	partía	partí
lograbas	_____	_____	_____	_____	_____
_____	_____	_____	_____	_____	_____
_____	_____	_____	_____	_____	_____
_____	_____	_____	_____	_____	_____
_____	_____	_____	_____	_____	_____

6. Fill out the sentences with the correct past form of the verb in brackets.

1. Colón *descubrió* (descubrir) América en 1492.
2. Sonia _____ (correr) media hora todas las mañanas antes de desayunar.
3. El verano pasado mis padres _____ (ir) de vacaciones al Caribe.
4. Les _____ (encantar) viajar en tranvía por la ciudad.
5. _____ (nosotros, comprar) un coche nuevo ayer por la tarde.

7. Make whatever corrections you consider necessary to produce correct sentences.

1. Tropezaba con la piedra y derramaba la leche.

   ➠ *Tropezó con la piedra y derramó la leche.*

2. Tuve miedo de la tormenta y fue a la cama de mis padres.

   _____

3. Siempre ordenaron la ropa antes de dormir.

   _____

4. Frió un huevo y lo comió rápidamente.

   _____

5. Nadaba por las mañanas en una piscina pero abandonó ese deporte.

   _____

8. Choose the correct alternative.

1. Picasso **pintó** / ~~pintaba~~ el *Guernica*.
2. Ayer no fui / iba a la playa porque llovió / llovía mucho.
3. El año pasado viajé / viajaba a Roma.
4. Cuando fui / era pequeña, me gustó / gustaba jugar en la arena.
5. Rosa estudió / estudiaba de noche.

29 WHAT DAY IS TODAY?
EXPRESSING THE TIME

- The most widespread time
preposition is **en**. This is used for
centuries, years, seasons, and
months, but not days or hours.

- Expressing the time now:

    *Estamos **en** el siglo XXI* (We're in the 21st century).
    *Estamos **en** (el año) 1369* (We are in the year 1369).
    *Estamos **en** primavera* (We're in spring).
    *Estamos **en** (el mes de) mayo* (We're in May).
    *Estamos **a** lunes / Hoy es lunes* (It's Monday).
    *Estamos **a** (día) diecisiete / Hoy es 17* (It's the 17th).
    *Son **las** tres* (It's three o'clock).
    *Es **la** una* (It's one o'clock).

- Expressing the time in the past / future:

    *La boda fue / será **en** el siglo XXI* (The wedding was / will be in the 21st century).
    *La boda fue **en** 1995 / será **en** 2010* (The wedding was in 1995 / will be in 2010).
    *La boda fue / será **en** verano* (The wedding was / will be in summer).
    *La boda fue / será **en** enero* (The wedding was / will be in January).
    *La boda fue / será **el** martes* (The wedding was / will be on Tuesday).
    *La boda fue / será **el** 18* (The wedding was / will be on the 18th).
    *La boda fue / será **a las** cuatro* (The wedding was / will be at four).

1. Choose the correct option for each sentence.

1. Estamos ~~a el~~ / *en el* siglo XXI.

2. Hoy empieza en / la primavera.

3. Estamos a / en 13 de abril.

4. Mi cumpleaños es en / el octubre.

5. Aún estamos en / a martes.

2. Express in which moment in time we are now.

1. Estamos *en el* siglo XXI.

2. Estamos _____ año 2005.

3. Estamos _____ invierno.

4. Estamos _____ mes de noviembre.

5. Estamos _____ domingo.

3. Fill each gap with one or more small words (articles, prepositions, etc.) when necessary.

1. Es un autor que (that) vivió *en* el primer milenio a.C. (BC).

2. Mi cumpleaños es _____ viernes.

3. _____ fines de semana voy a esquiar a una estación cerca de mi ciudad.

4. Estamos _____ marzo.

5. Son _____ 5:45 y nos esperan a la entrada del cine.

4. Make sentences in Spanish out of the following information.

1. This month / August. ➡ *Estamos en agosto.*

2. The elections / Thursday / 22 / April.

_____

3. We are / third millennium.

_____

4. She takes (recibe) yoga classes / Friday / four thirty.

_____

5. I saw her in the street / last Saturday.

_____

29

WHAT DAY IS TODAY?
EXPRESSING THE TIME

- Note certain differences between the way the time is expressed in English and Spanish:
  - Centuries in Spanish are indicated in Roman numbers.
  - Years are read like ordinary figures (e.g., *mil trescientos sesenta y nueve* for 1369).
  - Months and weekdays (like nationalities, languages, etc.) are not capitalized in Spanish, and the days of the month are cardinal numbers.
  - Most of the nouns related to time are masculine except: *estación* (season), *primavera* (spring), *semana* (week), *hora* (hour) and *fecha* (date).

ESTACIONES DEL AÑO (seasons of the year)	MESES DEL AÑO (months of the year)	DÍAS DE LA SEMANA (days of the week)
primavera (spring)	*enero* (January)	*lunes* (Monday)
verano (summer)	*febrero* (February)	*martes* (Tuesday)
otoño (autumn/fall)	*marzo* (March)	*miércoles* (Wednesday)
invierno (winter)	*abril* (April)	*jueves* (Thursday)
	mayo (May)	*viernes* (Friday)
	junio (June)	*sábado* (Saturday)
	julio (July)	*domingo* (Sunday)
	agosto (August)	
	septiembre (September)	
	octubre (October)	
	noviembre (November)	
	diciembre (December)	

- Days, numbers and weekdays, do not require any preposition. The days of the week in plural indicate regular activities and the singular forms are used for one off events (whether in the past or the future). Remember that no article is needed for stating which day of the week it is.
  - **General**:
    *Van al campo **los** domingos* (They go to the countryside on Sundays).
  - **Future**:
    *¿Quedamos **el** jueves (que viene)?* (Shall we meet next Thursday?)
  - **Statement**:
    Hoy es viernes, ayer fue jueves y mañana será sábado (Today is Friday, yesterday was Thursday and tomorrow will be Saturday).
  - **Past**:
    *Quedamos **el** jueves pasado* (We met last Thrusday).

5. Translate the following words without looking back at the unit.

1. Thursday ➡ *jueves*   Saturday _____   Tuesday _____

2. June _____   December _____   March _____

3. Autumn _____   Winter _____   Summer _____

4. Century _____   Millennium _____   Year _____

5. Season _____   Week _____   Date _____

6. Choose the correct gender for the following nouns.

1. L̶a̶ / El día.

2. La / El mes.

3. Las / Los estaciones.

4. La / El miércoles.

5. La / El fin de semana.

7. Make corrections to the following sentences if you find it necessary.

1. Fuimos de viaje (on a trip) en el Abril, no en el Marzo.

   ➡ *Fuimos de viaje en abril, no en marzo.*

2. Ayer fue el Miércoles, el tercer (third) día de la semana.

   _____

3. El Mayo es el mes de las flores.

   _____

4. El anuncio oficial del compromiso fue en 18, no en 19.

   _____

5. Los exámenes finales tienen lugar (take place) el mes de Junio.

   _____

8. Translate the following sentences into Spanish (writing the figures in words).

1. They arrived in March. ➡ *(Ellos/Ellas) llegaron en marzo.*

2. Summer is my favourite season of the year.

   _____

3. Juan visits Sara on Fridays.

   _____

4. That happened on September 23rd 1934.

   _____

5. I hate Mondays.

   _____

30 FIRST COME, FIRST SERVED
ORDINAL NUMBERS

- Ordinal numbers are used to indicate sequential order in a classification. The first twelve ordinal numbers are the following:

    primero (1st)

    segundo (2nd)

    tercero (3rd)

    cuarto (4th)

    quinto (5th)

    sexto (6th)

    séptimo (7th)

    octavo (8th)

    noveno (9th)

    décimo (10th)

    undécimo (11th)

    duodécimo (12th)

- From 13th onwards there is a pattern.

    decimotercero (13th)   *trigésimo* (30th)

    decimocuarto (14th)   *cuadragésimo* (40th)

    decimoquinto (15th)   *quincuagésimo* (50th)

    decimosexto (16th)   *sexagésimo* (60th)

    vigésimo (20th)   *septuagésimo* (70th)

    vigésimo primero (21st)   *octogésimo* (80th)

    vigésimo segundo (22nd)   *nonagésimo* (90th)

- All ordinals are variable both in gender and number depending on the noun they accompany (e.g., *noveno /novena /novenos /novenas*). Their short form varies for the masculine and feminine.

    1st – *1º /1ª*   3rd – *3º /3ª*

    2nd – *2º /2ª*   4th – *4º /4ª*

1. Match the two columns.

1. Primer	a) puestos
2. Segunda	b) curso
3. Primeros	c) piso
4. Sextas	d) puerta
5. Quinto	e) clasificadas

2. Write the following numbers in the correct form.

1. Seleccionamos a la *tercera* (3) candidata.
2. Comprasteis la _____ (5) parcela para hacer (in order to build) vuestra casa.
3. Es mi _____ (1) marido.
4. La suya fue la _____ (8) llamada de teléfono (phone call) en una hora.
5. Mi _____ (2) hija es muy alta para su edad.

3. Select an ordinal or a cardinal number for the following sentences.

1. Prestamos nuestros apuntes a una / ~~primera~~ compañera de clase (classmate).
2. Ponemos dos / el segundo montón de fotografías en el álbum.
3. Sirven tres / la tercera ronda de copas (round of drinks) a los invitados.
4. Suben siete / las séptimas plantas a pie (walking).
5. Mira cinco / la quinta estrella de la derecha (on the right hand side).

4. Translate the following sentences into Spanish.

1. We are celebrating our second anniversary.
   ➡ *Estamos celebrando nuestro segundo aniversario.*
2. This is the eleventh floor.
   _____
3. Picasso was born (nació) in the 19th century.
   _____
4. This is the first year I have holidays in the summer.
   _____
5. She introduced us to her third husband.
   _____

30

FIRST COME, FIRST SERVED
ORDINAL NUMBERS

- Ordinal numbers can appear either before or after a noun and they can also be alone if the name they refer to is clearly understood.

  Vamos al sexto piso / Vamos al piso sexto / Vamos al sexto

  (We go to the sixth floor).

- *Primero* (first) and *tercero* (third), when followed by a masculine noun, change to *primer* and *tercer*.

  *Mi coche es el **primero*** (My car is the first one).

  *El **primer** coche es nuestro* (The first car is ours).

  *Su piso es el **tercero*** (Their flat is the third).

  *Ellos viven en el **tercer** piso* (They live on the third floor).

- Partly due to their complexity, it is common that people use cardinal numbers after '10th', particularly for monarchs and centuries. For other entities, it is considered cultured to use the proper ordinal number.

  Isabel II (read: *Isabel segunda)* (Elizabeth the second).

  Alfonso XIII (read: *Alfonso trece)* (Alfonso the thirteenth).

  El siglo IV (read: *el siglo cuarto)* (the fourth century).

  El siglo XX (read: *el siglo veinte)* (the twentieth century).

- When an ordinal and a cardinal number appear together, the order in Spanish is the opposite to the English one (this is also the case with similar words that imply sequential order, like: *último* [last], *siguiente* [following], *próximo* [next], *previo/anterior* [previous], etc.).

  Las cinco primeras personas (the first five people).

  Los dos primeros libros (the first two books).

  Las seis últimas cosas (the last six things).

  Los tres siguientes capítulos (the three following chapters).

5. Provide the suitable full ordinal forms.

1. Uno nunca olvida su (1º) **primer** amor.
2. Las (2ªˢ) _____ partes nunca fueron buenas (popular saying meaning that sequels are never good).
3. A la (3ª) _____ vez va la vencida (popular saying equivalent of 'Third time lucky').
4. No hay (5º) _____ malo (popular pun meaning that the fifth item is never a bad one; probably because *quinto* is also an old-fashioned word for 'soldier').
5. Los últimos serán los (1ᵒˢ) _____ (popular saying meaning that the ones who are the last at present [the humble, etc.] will be the first [compensated] one day in the future).

6. Rewrite in full the following names and sequences.

1. Carlos I de España y V de Alemania (the Catholic Monarchs' grandson).
   ➡ **Carlos primero de España y quinto de Alemania.**
2. El siglo V a.C. _____
3. El siglo V d.C. _____
4. Una silla estilo Luis XV. _____
5. El romanticismo del siglo XIX. _____

7. Make whichever corrections you find necessary.

1. Las solistas primeras cantantes. ➡ **Las primeras cantantes solistas.**
2. La tercera y quinta plantas. _____
3. Los siguientes tres manifestantes. _____
4. La primera y diez concursantes. _____
5. Las previas tres citas. _____

8. Translate the following sentences into Spanish.

1. He/She prepared a big party for his/her 20th anniversary.
   ➡ **Preparó una gran fiesta para su vigésimo aniversario.**
2. The third exam is the most difficult one.

   _____
3. Our first date was unforgettable.

   _____
4. Their fifth son is the most intelligent.

   _____
5. The first four times I didn't get to the end.

   _____

MIAW, QUACK, TWEAT...
DIPHTHONGS AND TRIPHTHONGS

EL LEÓN ESTÁ
EN LA JAULA.

- In Spanish, a combination of a strong vowel (**a, e, o**) and a weak vowel (**i, u**) or of two weak vowels forms a diphthong if it is pronounced as one syllable. The stress falls on the strong vowel if there is one. In a combination of two weak vowels, it falls on the second element. If there is an **h** between the two vowels, it is still considered a diphthong.

*ci**u**dad* (town)	*a**u**la* (classroom)	*ni**e**ta* (granddaughter)
*p**ei**ne* (comb)	*a**i**re* (air)	*ja**u**la* (cage)
*a**hi**jado* (godson)	*a**hu**yentar* (to scare away)	*a**hu**mado* (smoked)

- When there are three vowels in one syllable, it is a triphthong. Most triphthongs are verbal forms.

  *limp**iái**s* (you clean)   *estud**iái**s* (you study)

- The **y** is similar to a vowel in both cases:

  *h**oy*** (today)   *Urug**uay*** (Uruguay)
  *m**uy*** (very)   *h**ay*** (there is/are)

- When two or three vowels go together but they are pronounced in different syllables, they are in **hiatus**. This is the case when an accent separates them or when they are all strong vowels:

*t**ea*** (torch)	*fa**e**na* (dirty trick)	*m**ea**ndro* (meander)
*f**eo*** (ugly)	*al**oe*** (aloe)	*a**ho**rros* (savings)

1. Classify these words as containing diphthongs or triphthongs.

cielo – ruido – Paraguay – miau – miedo – buey – peine

DIPHTHONGS	TRIPHTHONGS
cielo	_____
_____	_____
_____	_____
_____	

2. Decide if these words have diphthongs or hiatus.

veo – ahuecar – fea – vuelta – maorí – ahogar – polea – viudo

DIPHTHONGS	HIATUS
_____	*veo*
_____	_____
_____	_____
_____	_____

3. Complete the given words with the appropriate vowel combination:

au – áu – aú   ei – éi – eí   ia – ía – iá   ua – úa – uá

1. pausa
2. ___llan
3. r___da
4. p___ne
5. r___r
6. diecis___s
7. mom___
8. energ___
9. d___lisis
10. capic___
11. d___l
12. esc___lido

4. Correct the following sentences if necessary.

1. Tu tia espera en la estacion. ➡ *Tu tía espera en la estación.*
2. Sául corria detrás de una chica féa. _____
3. Caminabaís por los railes del tren. _____
4. En el rio habia una fuente de agua fresca. _____
5. Los estudiantes leian el periodico. _____

MIAW, QUACK, TWEAT...
DIPHTHONGS AND TRIPHTHONGS

- Diphthongs and triphthongs basically follow the same rules for orthographic accents as the rest of the words (see unit 21); however, the following rules must be taken into account:

  – When one of the vowels is strong, the accent is placed on this vowel:

escorp**ió**n (scorpion)	lecc**ió**n (lesson)
h**ué**sped (guest)	mir**ái**s (you look)
murci**é**lago (bat)	beb**éi**s (you drink)

  – If the diphthong involves two weak vowels, the accent is placed on the second one:

ac**uí**fero (aquifer)	interv**iú** (interview)

  – When a word with a final vocalic cluster ends in **y** and the stress falls on the last syllable, the word does not carry an accent:

jers**ey** (jumper)	car**ay** (gosh)

- Hiatus formed by two strong vowels follow the general rules for orthographic accents:

le**ó**n (lion)	ca**e**r (to fall)
po**e**ta (poet)	ca**ó**tico (chaotic)

- In the case of hiatus formed by a strong vowel plus a stressed weak vowel (**i** or **u**), this one always carries an accent, even if it would not be necessary according to general accent rules:

ca**í**da (fall)	le**í**do (read)
sonre**í**r (to smile)	ata**ú**d (coffin)
d**í**a (day)	pa**í**s (country)

- When the vowels in hiatus are **i** and **u**, the word does not carry an accent:

destr**ui**r (to destroy)	h**ui**da (escape)

5. Write the first person singular and the second person plural of the simple present of these verbs, paying attention to the accent.

1. Continuar ➟ *continúo – continuáis*
2. Averiguar _____ _____
3. Puntuar _____ _____
4. Evaluar _____ _____
5. Aguar _____ _____
6. Oír _____ _____
7. Reunir _____ _____

6. Decide if these words need an accent.

1. Ruido ➟ *ruido*
2. Guia _____
3. Despues _____
4. Via _____
5. Jaime _____
6. Prohibir _____
7. Fuente _____
8. Traicion _____
9. Lealtad _____

7. All these words carry an accent in the antepenultimate syllable. Add it to the correct vowel.

1. Periodico ➟ *periódico*
2. Acuifero _____
3. Nautico _____
4. Coagulo _____
5. Murcielago _____
6. Tuetano _____

8. Translate the following sentences into Spanish.

1. It is a deadly poison. ➟ *Es un veneno mortal / mortífero.*
2. You always change the place of things.
   _____
3. Running away is the easiest thing.
   _____
4. The disco has neon lights.
   _____
5. The trees have fallen.
   _____

32 MY NEIGHBOUR'S CAR IS BIGGER THAN MINE
SIMILES AND COMPARISONS

DUERME COMO UN TRONCO.

- The most common word to introduce a comparison in Spanish is **como** (like). There are idiomatic expressions involving comparisons which do not necessarily coincide in both languages.

   *Está durmiendo **como** un tronco* (He is sleeping like a log).

   *Canta **como** un ruiseñor* (He sings like a bird; literally: He sings like a nightingale).

   *Come **como** una lima* (He eats like a horse; no literal translation).

   *Estaba rojo **como** un tomate* (He was red as a beetroot; literally: He was red as a tomato).

- Comparing entities, actions, etc. in Spanish is far simpler than in English, because the form of words does not change. The words for 'more' and 'less' are **más** and **menos** respectively, and 'than' is **que**. Note that the type of personal pronoun used afterwards is the subject pronoun.

   *Aquella niña era **más** alegre **que** yo* (That girl was livelier than I was).

   *Come **menos** deprisa **que** sus hermanos* (He/she eats slower than his/her brothers and sisters).

- With numbers, **de** is used instead of *que*.

   *Queremos tener **más de** dos hijos* (We want to have more than two children).

   *Hacen **menos de** cinco cajas cada día* (They make less than five boxes each day).

1. Join each sentence in Spanish with its equivalent in English.

1. Se comportan como niños.
2. Ella es más divertida que tú.
3. Hoy tengo menos dinero que ayer.
4. Ellos corren más de diez kilómetros.
5. Eres fuerte como un león.

a) She is funnier than you.
b) You are as strong as a lion.
c) They behave like children.
d) Today I have less money than yesterday.
e) They run more than ten kilometres.

2. Write *como / que* to complete these sentences.

1. Gana tanto dinero *como* su marido.
2. Pedro es más alto _____ Luis.
3. Hoy no hace tanto calor _____ ayer.
4. Se ríe _____ una loca.
5. Este coche es menos caro _____ un Porsche.

3. Translate into English.

1. El río Miño no es tan ancho como el Nilo.
   ➧ *The Miño river is not as wide as the Nile.*
2. Londres es más grande que Madrid.
   _____
3. Cristina tiene más primos que Luis.
   _____
4. Los conejos corren más rápido que los gatos.
   _____
5. Esta semana hace más calor que la semana pasada.
   _____

4. Correct these sentences if necessary.

1. Ahora tiene un sueldo menos alto como el mío.
   ➧ *Ahora tiene un sueldo menos alto que el mío.*
2. Hoy hace más calor como ayer. _____
3. Tengo más que veinte alumnos. _____
4. Necesitamos más como diez sillas. _____
5. Es igual de rubio como su madre. _____

32 MY NEIGHBOUR'S CAR IS BIGGER THAN MINE
SIMILES AND COMPARISONS

- There are two ways to express the similarity between two or more entities. The first one is using **tan ... como** (as ... as), which is the most common one. When followed by a noun, *tan* becomes *tanto/tanta* or *tantos/tantas,* depending on the gender and number of the noun.

    *Están **tan** sorprendidos **como** los demás* (They are as surprised as the rest).

    *No es **tan** listo **como** su primo* (He is not as clever as his cousin).

    *Tengo **tanta** hambre **como** tú* (I am as hungry as you).

    *Juan compra **tantos** relojes **como** Pedro* (John buys as many watches as Peter).

- The second way of expressing similarity is: ***igual/iguales*...** or ***distinto/distinta/distintos/distintas*...** This is more emphatic.

    *Sois **iguales*** (You are identical).

    *Sois **iguales en** todo* (You are identical in everything).

    *Es **igual de** cabezota **que** su padre* (She is as stubborn as her father).

    *Son completamente **distintos de** los que vimos ayer* (They are completely different from the ones we saw yesterday).

- Note that in order to specify the aspect of the similarity, the preposition used with *igual* and *distinto* is **en**, unless it is an adjective, in which case it is **de**.

- If we want to introduce 'the most', we will have to use: ***el/la/los/las más*... de**. For 'the least' we use a similar construction: ***el/la/los/las menos*... de**. In both cases the choice of the article will depend on the gender and number of the noun it refers to.

    *Mi hermano es **el más** alto **de** la familia* (My brother is the tallest in the family).

    *Estas casas son **las más** baratas **de** la ciudad* (These houses are the cheapest in town).

    *María es **la menos** atractiva **de** todas sus hermanas* (María is the least attractive of all her sisters).

    *Esos cuadros son **los menos** caros **de** la tienda* (Those paintings are the least expensive in the shop).

- Finally, a common way of emphasizing a property or the manner in which an action is performed consists of adding ***-ísimo*** (and its related forms) to the word.

    Son inteligentísimas, así que lo acabaron rapidísimamente (They are highly intelligent, so they finished it very quickly).

5. Write in the correct form: *tan / tanto / tanta / tantos / tantas.*

1. Estoy ~~tan~~ cansado como tú.

2. No tiene _____ camisetas como mi hermano.

3. El monte Teide no es _____ alto como el Everest.

4. Hoy hace _____ viento como ayer.

5. Tengo _____ hermanos como Sara.

6. Use the correct preposition: *en / de.*

1. Son iguales ~~en~~ estatura.

2. Es igual _____ inteligente que su hermana.

3. No puedo comer más _____ dos helados.

4. Estos abrigos son diferentes _____ el precio.

5. Esta camisa es igual _____ cara que la chaqueta.

7. Cross out the word that is not correct.

1. Mi novio es el / ~~la~~ más simpático de todos.

2. Las dos hermanas son los / las más inteligentes de la clase.

3. María es el /la que estudia menos de la clase.

4. Esta casa es el / la más barata de toda la ciudad.

5. Los helados de chocolate son los /las menos ricos de la heladería.

8. Write a new sentence meaning the opposite.

1. Mi hijo es más alto que el suyo.

➠ *Mi hijo es menos alto que el suyo.*

2. Elena es menos inteligente que Manuel.

_____

3. Tengo tantos caramelos como tú.

_____

4. Tus hermanos son totalmente iguales.

_____

5. Es el chico menos atractivo que conozco.

_____

33 IS ANYBODY THERE?

INDEFINITE PRONOUNS AND DETERMINERS

- There is a heterogeneous group of pronouns which, unlike personal pronouns, demonstratives, possessives, etc., do not identify the referent (e.g. *Hay alguien durmiendo en mi cama* /There's somebody sleeping in my bed). In English these include 'somebody', 'anything', etc. In Spanish, there is no distinction between words starting with 'any-' and 'no-' (see unit 18) or between 'some' and 'any'.

PEOPLE	THINGS
alguien	algo
nadie	nada
cualquiera	
alguno/alguna/algunos/algunas	
ninguno/ninguna/ningunos/ningunas	
todo/toda/todos/todas	

- In order to deny the existence or presence of an entity, we use **nada** for things and **nadie** for people. They can go either at the beginning or end of the sentence. There is also another negative word, **ninguno**, both for things and people, which changes in gender and number: *ninguno/ninguna/ningunos/ningunas*.

  *No ocultaban **nada*** (They weren't hiding anything).

  *No me quiere **nadie*** (Nobody loves me).

  ***Nadie** me quiere* (Nobody loves me).

  *No quiero **ninguno*** (I don't want any).

1. Complete these sentences with a word like *alguien, nadie, cualquiera, alguno,* etc.

   1. No temo a *nadie*.

   2. Es tan fácil que puede ser director _____.

   3. ¿Hay _____ en casa (at home)?

   4. Tienen muchos amigos pero no llamó _____.

   5. _____ de sus hermanos está casado.

2. Do the same with *algo, nada, cualquier,* etc.

   1. Quiero *alguno* de esos libros.

   2. ¿Quieres beber _____?

   3. Es muy rara; _____ le gusta.

   4. ¡Que bonitas postales! Enviaré _____ a mis amigos.

   5. La película no me gustó _____.

3. Choose the correct word between the two options given.

   1. No me compro *nada* / ~~*nadie*~~.

   2. Alguno / alguien acaba de llegar.

   3. María tiene que comer algo / alguien

   4. Cualquier / cualquiera puede entrar en este restaurante.

   5. Eran muchos niños pero no entró ninguna / ninguno.

4. Write a new sentence meaning the opposite.

   1. No quiero nada más. ➡ *Quiero algo más.*

   2. Alguien está llamando a la puerta.

   _____

   3. Ellos tienen algún bolígrafo rojo.

   _____

   4. No compré ninguna falda.

   _____

   5. Nadie viene a la fiesta conmigo.

   _____

33 IS ANYBODY THERE?
INDEFINITE PRONOUNS AND DETERMINERS

- Indefinite pronouns can be modified and complemented like nouns.

    *Me contó **algo** muy divertido* (He told me something very funny).

    *No vino **nadie** de Manchester* (Nobody from Manchester came).

    *Tráeme **cualquier** cosa irrompible* (Bring me anything unbreakable).

- Some of these words can also modify nouns, like adjectives do. Note that all vary both in gender and number according to the noun they go with, except *bastante* (enough), which only varies in number. *Alguno, ninguno* and *cualquiera* become *algún, ningún* and *cualquier* before the noun.

    *Hay **pocos** sofás cómodos* (There are few comfortable sofas).

    *Vimos **muchas** mujeres bellas* (We saw many beautiful women).

    *Tengo **unas** ideas* (I have some ideas).

    *Tengo **algunas** ideas* (I have some ideas).

    *Llegamos a la **misma** solución* (We arrived at the same conclusion).

    ***Cualquier** opción es válida* (Any option is valid).

    *Una opción **cualquiera** es válida* (Any option is valid).

    *Teníamos **bastantes** razones* (We had enough reasons).

- Note that the difference between using **uno** and **alguno** (and their corresponding related forms) is almost imperceptible (see unit 6).

    *Tráeme **algunos** plátanos* (Bring me some bananas).

    *Tráeme **unos** plátanos* (Bring me some bananas).

- These words can appear together in the same phrase. The implications of some combinations and the relative order of the words are basically the same in both languages.

    *Quedan **pocas** naranjas* (There are few oranges left).

    *Quedan **unas pocas** naranjas* (There are a few oranges left).

    *Tengo **otras muchas** preguntas para ti* (I have many other questions for you).

    *Tú tienes **muchas menos*** (You have many less).

    *Pablo compró **bastante poco** hoy* (Paul has bought very little today).

5. Fill out the sentences with the correct word from the box.

pocas – bastante – algo – unos – cualquiera

1. Queremos comer *algo* rico.
2. Tengo _____ patatas, voy a comprar más.
3. No le sirve un coche _____.
4. Están llegando _____ barcos al puerto.
5. Queremos comer una sopa _____ picante.

6. Correct the following sentences.

1. ¿Tiene un periódico cualquier? ➡ ***¿Tiene un periódico cualquiera?***
2. Compré algunas discos. _____
3. Algo le regaló un ramo de flores. _____
4. No hay nadie en ese cajón. _____
5. Puedes invitar a alguienes a la fiesta. _____

7. Match the two lists of words.

1. Unas   a) coches
2. Bastantes   b) libros
3. Pocos   c) muñecas
4. Algunos   d) casa
5. Cualquier   e) cosas

8. Translate into Spanish the following sentences:

1. I am not in love with (estar enamorado de) anybody. ➡ ***No estoy enamorado de nadie.***
2. Some children play in the park. _____
3. Nobody lives in that house. _____
4. We listen to some records. _____
5. Can anybody help me? _____

34 NARCISSUS LOVES HIMSELF
REFLEXIVE AND EMPHATIC PRONOUNS

¡ ME DESPIDO !

- When the object of the action coincides with the subject, the pronouns used are the following:

> *Yo **me** lavo* (I wash myself).
>
> *Tú **te** lavas* (You wash yourself).
>
> *Él /Ella **se** lava* (He washes himself/herself).
>
> *Nosotros **nos** lavamos* (We wash ourselves).
>
> *Vosotros **os** laváis* (You wash yourselves).
>
> *Ellos **se** lavan* (They wash themselves).

- These pronouns are used for both the direct and the indirect objects.
  *Yo **me** compré un libro* (I bought myself a book / I bought a book for myself).

- Note that it is highly unlikely, for example, that a person sends a card to him/herself, so plural reflexives generally have the meaning of 'each other' or 'one another'. This can be expressed in other ways:

  *Vosotras **os** enviáis postales* (You send postcards to yourselves / one another).

  Se** saludaron **(los unos a los otros) (They greeted each other).

  *Lo hicieron **mutuamente*** (They did it reciprocally).

1. Join fragments from the three columns to create a sentence.

1. Yo   os sentís   con sus vecinos.

2. Nosotros   me peino   con el cuchillo.

3. Ellos   se cortó   en el sillón.

4. Vosotras   nos sentamos   con el cepillo.

5. Ella   se pelearon   muy halagadas.

2. Use the correct reflexive pronoun.

1. La niña *se* mira en el espejo.

2. _____ lastimé cuando abría la puerta.

3. ¿Por qué no _____ peinas con una coleta?

4. ¡No _____ escondáis de mí!

5. Los niños _____ están lavando las manos.

**3. Use an expression to complete the sentences expressing 'each other'
or 'one another'. (Be careful with the gender and the number.)**

1. Luis y Raúl se saludaron *mutuamente / el uno al otro.*

2. Los futbolistas se dieron masajes _____.

3. Marta y Cristina se ayudan _____.

4. Los novios se envían e-mails _____.

5. En la pelea, se lastimaron _____.

4. Use the correct reflexive pronoun.

1. **Me** / ~~mí~~ vestí con la ropa nueva.

2. Nos / os lavamos con agua fría.

3. Os / se ríen con ganas.

4. Mi abuela ya no se / te arregla como antes.

5. Se / te escondes detrás de la puerta.

34 NARCISSUS LOVES HIMSELF
REFLEXIVE AND EMPHATIC PRONOUNS

- There is a sequence that can be appended at the end of reflexive sentences: *a / para* / etc. + personal pronoun. *Mismo/misma/mismos/mismas* may be included for emphatic purposes.

> *Me hablo **a mí mismo/a*** (I talk to myself).
>
> *Te hablas **a ti mismo/a*** (You talk to yourself).
>
> *Se habla **a él/ella mismo/a*** (He/She talks to him/herself).
>
> *Nos hablamos **a nosotros/as mismos/as*** (We talk to ourselves).
>
> *Os habláis **a vosotros/as mismos/as*** (You talk to yourselves).
>
> *Se hablan **a sí mismos/as*** (They talk to themselves).

> *Lo hice **para mí*** (I did it for myself).
>
> *Escribe sólo **para sí misma*** (She writes only for herself).

- **Mismo** (and its related forms) can also be used right after the subject for emphatic (non-reflexive) purposes.

> *Lo hice **yo mismo*** (I did it myself).
>
> ***Él mismo** me lo dijo* (He himself said it to me).

- Not all the verbs that are reflexive in Spanish are also reflexive in English. There are verbs in Spanish that take a reflexive construction arbitrarily, i.e., with no reflexive meaning.

> ***Se** puso los pantalones* (He/she put his/her trousers on).
>
> ***Se** sentaron* (They sat down).
>
> ***Se** casó* (He/she got married).
>
> ***Os** marchasteis* (You left).
>
> *Tengo que cortar**me** el pelo* (I have to have my hair cut).

- Some of these verbs are also used without the reflexive pronoun when the action falls on another element.

> *El sacerdote casó a la pareja* (The priest married the couple).
>
> *Sienta al bebé en esa silla* (Sit the baby on that chair).
>
> *Estoy cortando un poco de pan* (I am cutting a bit of bread).

5. Use *mismo, misma, mismos, mismas* in the correct form.

1. Pedro se culpa (blames) a sí *mismo*.

2. María se peina ella _____.

3. Nos arreglamos (manage) bien nosotros _____.

4. Las niñas se visten ellas _____.

5. El bebé no puede comer por (by) sí _____.

6. Use the reflexive *se* when necessary.

1. Juan y Sara *se* casaron ayer.

2. _____ está cortando el pelo.

3. El obispo _____ casó a Felipe y Letizia.

4. _____ cortó dos trozos de queso.

5. La madre _____ sienta a la niña en su silla.

7. Translate the following sentences into Spanish.

1. My cousins are getting married this week.

➡ *Mis primos se casan esta semana.*

2. My little sister looks at herself in the mirror.

_____

3. I put my pyjamas on every night.

_____

4. Your friends left this morning.

_____

5. She cut herself with a knife.

_____

8. Correct the following sentences if necessary.

1. Se lo contó él misma. ➡ *Se lo contó él mismo / ella misma.*

2. Me calzamos nosotros mismos. _____

3. El cura se casó a los novios. _____

4. Ella canta para ti misma. _____

5. Vosotros misma lo podéis comprobar. _____

35 HOW LONG IS A RULER?
USEFUL DESCRIBING EXPRESSIONS

¿ CUÁNTOS AÑOS TIENES ?

- When describing or informing about events, places, things, people, etc., there are many useful expressions. One of them is **hay**, which corresponds to both 'there is' and 'there are'. Its past forms are **había** (continuous past) and **hubo** (simple past), both corresponding to 'there was' and 'there were'. Its future form, **habrá,** corresponds to 'there will be'.

> *Hay un hombre de pie fuera* (There is a man standing outside).
>
> *Hubo un maremoto la semana pasada* (There was a seaquake last week).
>
> *Había mucha gente en el aeropuerto* (There were many people at the airport).
>
> *Habrá alguien esperándote en la estación* (There will be someone waiting for you at the station).

- A somewhat similar verb, **hace,** is used impersonally before a noun or an adjective for the description of weather conditions. Its past forms are **hacía** (continuous past) and **hizo** (simple past), both corresponding to 'it was'. Its future form, **hará,** corresponds to 'it will be'. Another common verb in these descriptions is **está** *(estaba, estuvo, estará)*.

> *Hace bueno* (The weather is nice).
>
> *Hace viento* (It's windy).
>
> *Hará frío mañana* (It will be cold tomorrow).
>
> *Está nublado* (It's cloudy).
>
> *Está lloviendo* (It's raining).
>
> *Estaba brillando el sol* (The sun was shining).

1. Join each sentence in Spanish to its equivalent in English.

1. Hacía mucho calor dentro de la clase.
2. No había nadie en la estación.
3. Estará en la oficina toda la tarde.
4. Hay muchas cartas sobre la mesa.
5. Hizo mucho viento ayer.

a) There wasn't anybody at the station.
b) There are many letters on the table.
c) It was very windy yesterday.
d) It was very hot inside the class.
e) He/She will be at the office the whole afternoon.

2. Use the correct verb form: *hay, había, hubo, habrá,* to complete the following sentences.

1. **Hay** mucha fruta en la nevera.
2. _____ una vez una niña llamada Blancanieves (Snow White).
3. Hace muchos años _____ una iglesia aquí; ahora es un hotel.
4. _____ nuevos alumnos el curso que viene.
5. Ha llegado el invierno; ya no _____ más rosas en el jardín.

3. Complete the following sentences with *hace, hacía, hizo, hará*.

1. **Hace** mucho viento hoy.
2. Ayer _____ bastante calor.
3. Cuando yo era pequeña, no _____ tanto frío.
4. El verano que viene _____ buen tiempo.
5. Si no _____ mal tiempo, iremos a la playa.

4. Complete the sentences below with *hace* or *hay*.

1. **Hay** bastantes flores en el jardín.
2. _____ pocos días encontré a tu padre en la calle.
3. No _____ sitio para más cuadros.
4. Juan dice que hoy no _____ periódico.
5. ¡ _____ un tiempo espantoso!

35

HOW LONG IS A RULER?
USEFUL DESCRIBING EXPRESSIONS

- The expression of time also shows certain differences between English and Spanish. As seen in unit 10, **llevar** (which in other contexts can also mean 'to take' or 'to carry') is a very common verb used to indicate temporal duration, and is directly followed by the time word or expression. In the present it is frequently translated by 'to be' in the present perfect ('have/has been'). In the past it is translated by 'had been'. It can also appear in the progressive form.

   *¿Cuántos años **llevas** de policía en Washington? / ¿Cuántos años **hace** que eres policía en Washington?* (How long have you been a policeman in Washington?)

   *Los ejecutivos **llevan** una hora discutiendo / Los ejecutivos **hace** una hora que discuten / están discutiendo (*The executives have been arguing for an hour).

   ***Llevaba** un año pidiéndole que se casara con él* (He had been asking her to marry him for a year).

- When describing people, moods, objects, etc., and whether we like them or not, it is common to find a lack of equivalence between both languages.

   ***Estás** radiante* (You look radiant). (See unit 11.)

   ***Tengo** sueño* (I am sleepy; literally: *I have sleep).

   *¿Cuántos años **tenía**? **Tenía** 25 años* (How old was he/she? He/she was 25 years old; literally: *He/she had 25 years).

   ***Teníamos** sed* (We were thirsty; literally: *We had thirst).

   *¿Cuánto **miden**? **Miden** un metro de largo* (How long are they? They are one metre long; literally: *How much do they measure? They measure one metre of long).

   *¿**Cuánto** cuestan esos pendientes? –Diez euros* (How much do those earrings cost? –Ten euros).

   *No **nos gustan** mucho* (We don't like them very much).

   ***Me encanta** la paella* (I love paella).

5. Change these sentences using *hace* or a form of *llevar*.

1. Hace tres años que vivo en Barcelona. ➠ *Llevo tres años viviendo en Barcelona.*

2. Él lleva trabajando aquí un mes.

   _____

3. Hace poco tiempo que están casados.

   _____

4. Llevan mucho tiempo enfermos.

   _____

5. Luisa lleva media hora hablando.

   _____

6. Select the correct form of the two options given.

1. No tengo / ~~estoy~~ hambre.
2. Lleva el paraguas. Hace / está lloviendo.
3. Hace / Lleva un mes estudiando español.
4. Hace / Lleva un año que no duermo bien.
5. Está / Tiene más edad de la que aparenta.

7. Translate the following sentences into Spanish.

1. Are you hungry today? ➠ *¿Tienes hambre hoy?*
2. I am tired and sleepy.

   _____

3. My brother is twenty years old.

   _____

4. How long is the ruler? It is fifty centimetres long.

   _____

5. The children are very thirsty.

   _____

8. Correct the following sentences if necessary.

1. Los trabajadores hacen dos semanas en huelga.

   ➠ *Los trabajadores llevan dos semanas en huelga.*

2. Lleva mucho tiempo que no te veía. _____

3. Hacía muchas bicicletas en el parque. _____

4. Está un día precioso. _____

5. Llevan mucha gente en la playa. _____

36 ¿QUÉ SERÁ, SERÁ?
THE FUTURE TENSE

ALGÚN DÍA SERÉ BOMBERO.

- The uses of the future in Spanish are similar to those in English: it expresses states or actions that are expected but have not taken place yet. The regular conjugation for the standard future tense is as follows.

-AR	-ER	-IR
Yo dar**é**	Yo ofrecer**é**	Yo pedir**é**
Tú dar**ás**	Tú ofrecer**ás**	Tú pedir**ás**
Él dar**á**	Él ofrecer**á**	Él pedir**á**
Nosotros dar**emos**	Nosotros ofrecer**emos**	Nosotros pedir**emos**
Vosotros dar**éis**	Vosotros ofrecer**éis**	Vosotros pedir**éis**
Ellos dar**án**	Ellos ofrecer**án**	Ellos pedir**án**

*Mañana **iré** al colegio en autobús* (Tomorrow I'll go to school by bus).

*El presidente **dará** un discurso la semana que viene* (The president will give a speech next week).

*El verano que viene **viajarán** a Australia* (Next summer they will travel to Australia).

- Note that the future forms of all three conjugations are identical and that the verbs corresponding to all but the first person plural take an orthographic accent.

    *Algún día **elaboraremos** el árbol genealógico de la familia* (Someday we'll do the family tree).

    ***Celebraremos** mi cumpleaños el sábado* (We will celebrate my birthday next Saturday).

1. Complete the following sentenceswith the correct future form of the verb in brackets.

1. Mañana el grupo (actuar) **actuará** en Madrid.

2. Nosotros (llegar) _____ en el tren de las diez.

3. Vosotros os (encontrar) _____ en el bar.

4. Los partidos (acabar) _____ muy tarde.

5. ¿Me (ayudar) _____ usted con el trabajo?

2. Match the two columns to form correct and logical sentences.

1. Sara y Cristina   a) estudiaré toda la noche.

2. Los niños   b) participará en el concurso.

3. Nuestro amigo   c) estará en el taller toda la semana.

4. El coche   d) prepararán la fiesta sorpresa.

5. Yo   e) jugarán al escondite.

3. Fill out the sentences with the correct word from the box.

> jubilará – durará – lloverá – llegaremos – comeré

1. Mi padre se **jubilará** dentro de cinco años.

2. La película _____ tres horas.

3. Me _____ toda la tarta.

4. _____ el próximo viernes.

5. Han anunciado que _____ toda la noche.

4. Translate the following sentences into Spanish.

1. We will eat at home on Friday.

   ➠ *Comeremos en casa el viernes. / El viernes comeremos en casa.*

2. Next year John will finish his career.

   _____

3. They will visit their parents at the weekend.

   _____

4. I will start my exams next week.

   _____

5. You will win the race.

   _____

36

¿QUÉ SERÁ, SERÁ?
THE FUTURE TENSE

- The future form can also be used to express something which is possible and even probable, but about which there is no absolute certainty.

    Serán *las diez* (It must be ten o'clock).

    Tendrá *mucho dinero pero no lo demuestra* (He may have a lot of money, but he doesn't show it).

- There is another way to express the future when this is imminent, close in time, and the speaker is confident of the possibilities of the given state or action. It is formed with the simple present of the verb *ir* (to go) + *a* + infinitive. It is a similar structure to the 'going to' future in English.

    Van a analizar *la situación cuidadosamente* (They're going to analyse the situation carefully).

    Vais a ir *de vacaciones con vuestro jefe* (You're going to go on holidays with your boss).

- As seen in unit 10, it is also possible to use the simple present to refer to a future action with 'absolute' certainty, such as events related to official calendars and timetables.

    El avión **sale** *mañana a las tres* (The plane leaves tomorrow at three o'clock).

    Los Juegos Olímpicos **empiezan** *dentro de un mes* (The Olympic Games will begin in a month's time).

    Este año **acaba** *en martes* (This year will end on a Tuesday).

- The present simple is also used when the future action is seen as immediate.

    Ahora mismo **voy** (I'm coming).

    Llega *dentro de un momento* (He'll be here in a moment).

    Vuelve *para la cena* (She'll be back for supper).

- By extension it is also used for actions which we are sure will definitely happen.

    Mi padre **se jubila** *el mes que viene* (My father will retire next month).

- The most common prepositions that introduce a period of time in the future are **dentro de** and **en** (see unit 29). They are interchangeable.

    Iré **en** */* **dentro de** *un mes* (I'll go in a month's time).

5. Choose an appropriate option for each sentence.

1. Juan va / ~~irá~~ al cine esta tarde (ya tiene los billetes).

2. La bolsa está muy llena y se va a romper / romperá (es probable).

3. Voy a comer / comeré sardinas para cenar (tengo esa intención).

4. El tren saldrá / sale dentro de unos segundos (inmediatamente).

5. Sergio y Elena llegan / llegarán sobre (around) las seis (no es seguro).

6. Complete the sentences below with *ir a* + verb.

1. Pedro va a llegar (llegar) tarde.

2. Nosotros _____ (salir) de compras.

3. El programa _____ (comenzar).

4. Mi familia _____ (viajar) a Italia.

5. Las plantas _____ (secarse).

7. Use the simple present to complete these sentences. Choose the correct verb from *tener, empezar, reunirse, abrir, llegar*.

1. El tribunal se reúne mañana.

2. La película _____ dentro de cinco minutos.

3. El avión _____ un retraso de media hora.

4. Mis amigos _____ pasado mañana en tren.

5. La exposición _____ a las cuatro y cuarto.

8. State whether these sentences express a certainty or a possibility.

1. Tendrá unos cuarenta años. ⇒ POSSIBILITY.

2. La sesión terminará a las cuatro. ⇒ _____

3. Nunca conoceré la verdad. ⇒ _____

4. Serán las doce, más o menos. ⇒ _____

5. Te compraré un traje nuevo. ⇒ _____

37 UNTIL THE END OF TIME

MORE TIME EXPRESSIONS

- In unit 29 some standard forms to state past, present and future actions were presented. This must be completed as follows.

  - **For the past:**
    ayer (yesterday)
    antes de ayer (the day before yesterday)
    la semana pasada (last week)
    el mes /el año pasado (last month / year)

  - **For the present:**
    hoy (today)

  - **For the future:**
    mañana (tomorrow)
    pasado mañana (the day after tomorrow)
    la semana /el mes /el año que viene (next week / month / year)

    *Mis padres llegaron **ayer*** (My parents arrived yesterday).
    *Mis padres llegan **hoy*** (My parents arrive today).
    *Mis padres llegarán **mañana*** (My parents will arrive tomorrow).

- Notice that 'morning' and 'tomorrow' correspond to the same word in Spanish: **mañana**.

    *Ellos llegan **mañana*** (They arrive tomorrow).
    *El curso termina **por la mañana*** (The course finishes in the morning).

1. Complete the sentences with the correct word from the box.

> ayer – mañana – hoy – antes de ayer – pasado mañana

1. Mis amigos llegarán *mañana / pasado mañana.*
2. Las clases terminaron _____
3. _____ hace un día lluvioso.
4. Jaime vendrá a comer _____
5. Su madre se marchó _____

2. Decide if the word *mañana* in the following sentences means 'tomorrow' or 'morning'.

1. Las clases se terminan mañana. ➡ TOMORROW.
2. Dijeron que llamarían por la mañana. ➡ _____
3. Saldremos de viaje a media mañana. ➡ _____
4. Tiene turno de mañana en el hospital. ➡ _____
5. Mañana se espera un día soleado. ➡ _____

3. Change the tense of the sentences using the words in brackets.

1. Hoy hace mucho calor (mañana). ➡ *Mañana hará mucho calor.*
2. Pasado mañana cenaremos juntos (antes de ayer).

   _____
3. Ayer fue mi cumpleaños (hoy). _____
4. Mañana iremos a la ópera (ayer). _____
5. Antes de ayer terminé las clases temprano (pasado mañana).

   _____

4. Translate the following sentences into Spanish.

1. Spring begins tomorrow. ➡ *La primavera empieza mañana.*
2. Today is Monday. _____
3. The film was released yesterday. _____
4. I will wake up early tomorrow morning. _____
5. The day before yesterday it was snowing all day.

   _____

153

37

UNTIL THE END OF TIME
MORE TIME EXPRESSIONS

- As mentioned in unit 12, there is a mismatch between the parts of the day in English and Spanish.

  Mañana ⟹ It is common to refer to it from 1.00 a.m. up to lunchtime, which in Spain, for example, is typically between 2.00 and 2.30 p.m.

  Tarde ⟹ It is equivalent both to 'afternoon' and 'evening' and lasts until around 9.00 p.m.

  Noche ⟹ It lasts until 12.00 p.m.

  Madrugada ⟹ It refers to the period between 1.00 and 5.00 a.m. approximately.

- In order to refer to a part of any day, past, present, or future, the part is introduced by the preposition *por*. A common word for *ayer por la noche* (yesterday night) is **anoche** (last night).

  *Me iré a esquiar mañana **por la tarde*** (I'll go skiing tomorrow afternoon).

  *Antes de ayer **por la noche** vi una película* (The day before yesterday in the evening I saw a film).

  *Mi hijo adolescente vino **anoche** tardísimo* (My teenage son came very late last night).

- We also refer to a part of today with the demonstrative **este** and its related forms.

  ***Esta mañana** hacía mucho frío* (It was very cold this morning).

  ***Esta tarde** participaremos en un concurso* (This afternoon we'll participate in a contest).

  ***Esta noche** iremos al cine* (Tonight we are going to the cinema).

- The standard preposition to refer to a period of time, past, present or future, is **durante** (for / during).

  *El bebé se despertó diez veces **durante** la noche* (The baby woke up ten times during the night).

  *Estuve trabajando en la embajada **durante** diez años* (I worked in the embassy for ten years).

- As seen above, for 'last' and 'next', in Spanish the words *pasado* and *próximo / que viene* (and their related forms) are used respectively.

  *La escuela terminó la semana **pasada*** (School finished last week).

  *María se casará el mes **que viene*** (María will get married next month).

5. Match the parts of the day with the corresponding time.

1. Mañana   a) 11.00 p.m.
2. Tarde   b) 10.30 a.m.
3. Noche   c) 2.00 a.m.
4. Madrugada   d) 6.00 p.m.

6. Correct the following sentences according to the data in brackets, if necessary.

1. Mañana por la mañana vamos al médico. (5 p.m.)

   ➠ *Mañana por la tarde vamos al médico.*

2. Esta tarde iremos a bailar. (11.00 p.m.)

   _____

3. Me gusta dormir la siesta por la tarde. (4 p.m.)

   _____

4. El avión llegó de tarde. (4 a.m.)

   _____

5. Voy a ver a mi novio por la noche. (7 p.m.)

   _____

7. Complete the sentences with the words from the box.

por la mañana – durante – esta – anoche – la semana pasada

1. Llegaron de viaje justo *anoche*.
2. La tienda abre temprano _____
3. _____ tarde nos vemos.
4. _____ terminó el invierno.
5. Han vivido en esta casa _____ diez años.

8. Translate the following sentences into Spanish.

1. They will leave at dawn. ➠ *Se irán al amanecer.*
2. We will prepare the cake this morning. _____
3. I'll see you tomorrow evening. _____
4. I've worked a lot the whole week. _____
5. You went to Rome last year. _____

38

WHERE IS THE ROYAL PALACE?

ASKING FOR AND GIVING DIRECTIONS

- To ask for directions of where places are or how to get to a particular place, the basic question starts with **dónde** (where). (See unit 19.)

  *¿**Dónde** está la estación de autobuses?* (Where is the bus station?)

  *¿**Dónde** hay un supermercado?* (Where is there / can I find a supermarket?)

- These questions can be preceded by polite formulae such as:

  ¿Puede decirme...?   *¿Podría indicarme...?*

  *¿Puede decirme **dónde** está el hospital?* (Can you tell me where the hospital is?)

  *¿Podría indicarme **dónde** hay una farmacia?* (Could you tell me where I can find a chemist's?)

- Note that in Spanish the order of words is not altered in indirect questions.

- There are other ways of asking for specific instructions of how to get to a place. All of them can be preceded by the polite formulae indicated above.

  *¿**Cómo se va** a la playa?* (How do I get to the beach?)

  *¿**Cómo se llega** a la Calle Mayor?* (How do I get to the Main Street?)

- Another useful expression to ask for a place is: *Perdone, estoy buscando...*

  Perdone, estoy buscando la Calle Real (Excuse me, I'm looking for Real Street).

1. Make the following questions more polite.

1. ¿Dónde está el hospital? ➡ *¿Podría indicarme, por favor, dónde está el hospital?*

2. ¿Cómo se va al teatro? _____

3. ¿Dónde hay un banco? _____

4. ¿Cómo llego hasta el aeropuerto? _____

5. ¿Cómo se va a la Avenida de Europa? _____

2. Write adequate questions for these answers (include the word given in brackets).

1. ¿_____?
   Para ir a casa de Pedro tienes que tomar el autobús número 5. (llegar)

2. ¿_____?
   Mi casa nueva está cerca del parque. (dónde)

3. ¿_____?
   Tiene que torcer a la derecha, la panadería está al fondo de la calle. (indicar)

4. ¿_____?
   Para ir a la peluquería bajas la calle y giras por la segunda a la izquierda. (cómo)

5. ¿_____?
   La Plaza de España está al fondo de esa calle. (perdón)

3. Translate into Spanish.

1. Can you tell me how to get to the airport?
   ➡ *¿Puede decirme cómo ir / llegar al aeropuerto?*

2. Where is the post office, please?
   _____

3. How do I get to the football stadium?
   _____

4. Excuse me, I'm looking for a travel agency.
   _____

5. Could you tell me how to get to the port?
   _____

4. Make up correct questions asking for directions with these prompts.

1. haber / pastelería ➡ *¿Sabe usted si hay alguna pastelería por aquí?*

2. llegar / aeropuerto ➡ _____

3. estar / biblioteca ➡ _____

4. ir / cine ➡ _____

5. estar / hotel Majestic ➡ _____

38 WHERE IS THE ROYAL PALACE?
ASKING FOR AND GIVING DIRECTIONS

- Directions are usually given using the imperative form of the verbs.

    Gire a la izquierda/derecha (Turn left/right).

    Tome el primer cruce a la derecha (Take the first crossing on the right).

    Tome la primera (calle) a la izquierda y luego la segunda a la derecha (Take the first [street] on the left and then the second on the right).

    Siga todo recto hasta el semáforo (Go straight on to the traffic lights).

- Other common expressions which you can hear with the reply are:

    No tiene pérdida (You can't miss it).

    Puede atajar por el parque (You can take a short-cut across the park).

    Pregunte otra vez al llegar a la iglesia (Ask again when you get to the church).

- When you give or are given a specific address, bear in mind that in Spanish the number of the house (building) goes after the name of the street, and that the floor is shown in ordinal numbers, and the flat by a letter or words like *izquierda* (left) or *derecha* (right).

    Tienes que ir a la calle Pablo Picasso 5, 3º A (You have to go to 5 Pablo Picasso Street, 3rd A).

    Vivo en la calle Gran Vía 22, 5º D (I live at 22 Gran Vía, 5th D).

- The abreviations of *DRCHA* (right) or IZDA/*IZQDA* (left) are often used in written addresses. Most addresses contain the words *calle* (street), *avenida* (avenue), *carretera* (road) or *plaza* (square).

    Estamos en la plaza de la Constitución 4, 5º drcha. (We are at 4 Constitution Square, 5th floor on the right).

    Para ir al cine tenemos que tomar la avenida de América (To go to the cinema we have to take America Avenue).

MÉXICO D. F.

1. Catedral
2. Palacio Nacional
3. Sede del Gobierno del Distrito Federal
4. Anexo del Gobierno del Distrito Federal
5. Hotel de la Ciudad de México
6. Nacional Monte de Piedad
7. Secretaría de Educación Pública
8. Colegio de San Ildefonso
9. Ruinas del Templo Mayor
10. Museo del Templo Mayor
11. Ex-templo de Santa Teresa
12. Ex-Arzobispado
13. Museo José Luis Cuevas
14. Academia de San Carlos
15. Suprema Corte de Justicia
16. Museo de la Ciudad de México
17. Templo de Jesús de Nazareth
18. Ex-templo de San Agustín
19. Casa de los Condes de San Mateo Valparaíso
20. Templo de La Profesa
21. Biblioteca del Congreso
22. Asamblea de Representantes del Distrito Federal
23. Ex-Aduana
24. Templo de La Enseñanza

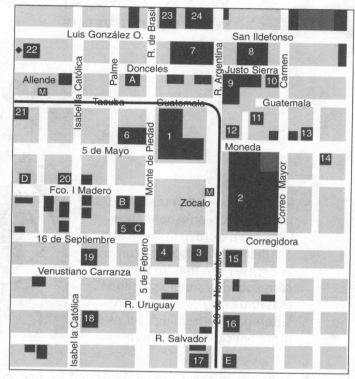

HOTELES:
A. Catedral **
B. Majestic ****
C. Gran Hotel ****
D. Ritz ****
E. Castropol **

5. Describe in Spanish the route followed by the grey line mentioning all the important places you pass by.

6. Explain how to get to *las ruinas del Templo Mayor* (9) from *la ex-Aduana* (23).

7. Explain how to get to *la catedral* (1) from *Casa de los Condes* (19).

8. Complete the following conversation at the Ritz Hotel.

P: Por favor, ¿podría _____ cómo se va al Palacio Nacional?

S: Sí, cómo no. Tiene que _____ por esta calle _____ el Zócalo.

Allí _____ a la izquierda y luego a la _____, rodeando el Zócalo. Allí verá usted el Palacio _____.

P: _____ por su ayuda.

YOU'LL HAVE TO MAKE DO WITH THIS LESSON
SOME USEFUL VERBS

- It is common to find that there is not a perfect correspondence between a word in Spanish and another one in English. In units 10 and 37 we saw that 'to be' may correspond to *ser* or *estar* and that *tarde* may correspond to 'afternoon' or 'evening'. Let us see other typical contrastive cases.

- The verb 'to know' can be translated as ***conocer*** and ***saber*** (both irregular). The former is more intuitive and used with people, places, situations, etc., and is typically followed by a noun. The latter is used for academic disciplines and skills, and may be followed by a noun or an infinitive. It is equivalent to 'know how to' or 'can'.

  *¿**Sabéis** dónde está el museo?* (Do you know where the museum is?)

  ***Conocéis** a la gente de esta región* (You know the people from this region).

  ***Conozco** este lugar muy bien* (I know this place very well).

  ***Sabe** hablar varios idiomas* (She can speak several languages).

- ***Saber*** can appear with the type of complements of ***conocer*** in constructions like: *saber lo que* and *saber cómo*, implying a deep knowledge of what follows.

  ***Sé lo que** necesitas* (I know what you need).

  ***Sabes cómo** son los vecinos de esta comunidad* (You know what the neighbours are like in this block of flats).

1. Join each sentence in Spanish with its equivalent in English.

1. Él conoce a todas las personas del pueblo.
2. Ella sabe hablar japonés.
3. Conocemos esta ciudad muy bien.
4. Mi amiga sabe cómo llegar al museo.
5. Yo sé lo que es pasar frío.

a) I know what it means to be cold.
b) We know this city very well.
c) He knows everybody in this village.
d) She can speak Japanese.
e) My friend knows how to get to the museum.

2. Use the correct form of *saber* or *conocer* in the sentences below.

1. No *sé* hablar ruso.
2. Mi profesora _____ bien a mis padres.
3. _____ que (that) te quiero mucho.
4. Algunos jóvenes no _____ cómo portarse en clase.
5. Juan _____ muchas culturas.

3. Translate the following sentences into Spanish using a form of *saber*. Be careful! It is an irregular verb.

1. My sister can play the piano very well. ➡ *Mi hermana sabe tocar el piano muy bien.*
2. I don't know how to open this box. _____
3. Do you know where my suitcase is? _____
4. We can't do this exercise. _____
5. My friends can't speak English. _____

4. Translate into Spanish the sentences below using a form of *conocer*. Be careful! It is an irregular verb.

1. I don't know your brother. ➡ *No conozco a tu hermano.*
2. My parents know this city a little. _____
3. Don't you know me? I'm your mother! _____
4. I am very familiar with his last book. _____
5. Mary doesn't know Madrid. _____

39 YOU'LL HAVE TO MAKE DO WITH THIS LESSON
SOME USEFUL VERBS

- Sometimes two verbs in English are translated by just one in Spanish. 'Do' and 'make' are translated by **hacer** in all situations. As seen in unit 35, *hacer* is also used when talking about the weather.

  *Los estudiantes **hacen** los exámenes en junio* (Students take their exams in June).

  *Pedro **hace** su cama todas las mañanas* (Peter makes his bed every morning).

  *¿Qué tiempo **hará** mañana?* (What will the weather be like tomorrow?)

- Another problematic verb is **encontrar**. It is translated as 'to find' for things (e.g., that were lost) and 'to meet' for people (e.g., by chance in the street, etc.). However, if you meet somebody for the first time, you use *conocer*.

  *No **encuentro** mis gafas* (I can't find my glasses).

  *Nos **encontramos** con/a tu prima en el metro* (We met your cousin in the underground).

  *Ayer **conocí** a la mujer de mi vida* (Yesterday I met the woman of my life).

- Note that in the second sentence *encontrar* is reflexive and can take the preposition **con** or **a**. **A** is used due to the personal object (see unit 2).

- *Encontrar* is also used to express opinion, to indicate location and, as a reflexive verb, in sentences about health with the meaning of 'feel'.

  ***Encuentro** tus comentarios muy interesantes* (I find your comments very interesting).

  ***Me encuentro** delante del Taj Mahal* (I am in front of the Taj Mahal).

  *¿Qué tal **se encuentra** usted hoy?* (How do you feel today?)

- Although two or more words may have practically the same meaning, one of them may be preferred over the others in a given context.

  For example, *hacer, realizar, llevar a cabo, elaborar* and *desarrollar*.

  Hacer is the most generic of this series and the rest have a formal register; of these, the last two, *elaborar* and *desarrollar* allude to the creation process apart from the result, and they are used for real accomplishments. Finally, *desarrollar* is used in the language of computing.

  *El programador **ha desarrollado** una nueva interfaz* (The programmer has developed a new interface).

5. Fill out the sentences below with the correct word from the box.

> encuentra – conocerá – hace – hizo – encontré

1. Ayer **hizo** mucho calor, pero por la noche llovió.
2. Me _____ con mi profesora de francés en el autobús.
3. Mañana _____ a la mujer de su hermano.
4. Víctor se _____ mal desde ayer.
5. _____ más de un año que no lo veo.

6. Match the two columns to form a sentence, adding the appropriate form of the verb *hacer*.

1. Tengo que **hacer**
2. _____ mucho frío
3. Los deportistas _____
4. Mañana _____
5. Ellos _____ las maletas

a) una hora antes de marcharse.
b) un día muy soleado.
c) muchos deberes de matemáticas.
d) esta mañana.
e) mucho ejercicio.

7. Translate the following sentences into Spanish using a form of *encontrar*. Be careful! It is an irregular verb.

1. I didn't find the book that (que) you wanted. ⟹ **No encontré el libro que querías.**
2. I feel much better today, thank you.

_____

3. We will meet you at the cinema tomorrow.

_____

4. If you are looking for a present, you will find it in this shop.

_____

5. They will never find that manuscript, it is very rare.

_____

8. Complete the following sentences with a form of *conocer* or *encontrar*.

1. Ayer **conocí** al novio de Isabel. Es muy agradable.
2. Mi marido no se _____ bien, no va a ir a trabajar hoy.
3. ¡Los hombres nunca _____ las cosas en casa!
4. No _____ a nadie que cante como Pavarotti.
5. Se _____ en un viaje a Madrid.

40 IF I WERE A RICH MAN...
CONDITIONAL SENTENCES

- In Spanish, like in English, we use conditional sentences to talk about a situation that might possibly happen and to say what its results might be.

- In Spanish the most frequent word used to introduce a condition is **si** (if).

    Si *llueve mañana, no podremos ir a la playa.* (If it rains tomorrow, we won't be able to go to the beach).

    *Te llamaré **si** te necesito.* (I'll call you if I need you).

- Like in English, the condition may appear in any position in the sentence. If it comes at the beginning, it is always followed by a comma. Note also that **si** does not take an accent; **sí** with an accent is an affirmative or a personal pronoun (see unit 21).

- We can use conditionals in several cases: to mention events and situations that often happen, that may happen in the future, that could have happened in the past but did not happen, or that are impossible to happen at all.

- When we talk about events which may possibly happen in the future, we use a future tense in the main part of the sentence.

    *Si te casas con Luis, no **serás** feliz* (If you marry Luis, you will not be happy).

    ***Aprobarás** el examen si estudias* (You'll pass the exam if you study).

1. Match the two parts of the sentence.

1. Nos visitará
2. Si viene mi tío,
3. Puedo prestarte dinero
4. Si llegas pronto,
5. Pedro puede ayudarte

a) nos llevará a la playa.
b) si tiene tiempo.
c) si no te arreglas (manage) sola.
d) si no te llega para la entrada.
e) podemos tomar un café.

2. Put the verbs in brackets in the appropriate form.

1. Si los niños *se portan* (portarse) mal, su madre los castigará.
2. Si le preguntas a Elena, te _____ (explicar) ese problema.
3. No podrás entrar si no _____ (tener) tu reserva.
4. Te _____ (gustar) más la ópera si conoces el argumento.
5. Hablaré con el jefe si lo _____ (encontrar) en la oficina.

3. Correct the following sentences if necessary.

1. Cantaré en el festival si no me dolerá la garganta. ⮑ *...si no me duele la garganta.*
2. Si lo piensas un poco, solucionaste el problema. _____
3. Toman el tren si se darán prisa. _____
4. Compran peras si les llegará (have enough) el dinero. _____
5. Si prestan atención, reconocerán este cuadro. _____

4. Translate the following sentences into Spanish.

1. If you are a good girl, I'll take you to the cinema.
   ⮑ *Si eres una buena chica, te llevaré al cine.*
2. If I pass my exams, I will travel to France.
   _____
3. I'll lend you my book if you promise to look after it.
   _____
4. Martha will come with us if we invite her.
   _____
5. If the weather is good, we'll go walking.
   _____

- When we talk about situations and events that are expected to happen when the condition is fulfilled (such as universal truths, scientific facts, habits, etc.), we use the present in both parts of the sentence.

  Si el agua se calienta a 100 grados, **hierve**. (If water is heated up to 100 degrees, it boils).

  Si hace calor, **ponemos** *el aire acondicionado.* (If it is hot, we switch on the air conditioning).

- In these situations, we can also use **cuando** (when) or **siempre que** (whenever) instead of *si*.

  Siempre que *leo en el coche, me mareo* (Whenever I read in the car, I feel sick).

  Vamos a esquiar **cuando** *nieva en febrero* (We go skiing when it snows in February).

- We can see that a slightly different meaning can be conveyed just by changing the verb tense.

  Si hace buen tiempo el domingo, **vamos** *a la playa* (If the weather is good on Sundays, we go to the beach: We always go to the beach when the weather is good on a Sunday).

  Si hace buen tiempo el domingo, **iremos** *a la playa* (If the weather is good this coming Sunday, we'll go to the beach).

- By extension, a similar type of construction can also be used to give advice, ask somebody to do us a favour, make a suggestion, etc. In these cases the main verb is an imperative.

  Si no te encuentras bien, **vete** *al médico.* (If you don't feel well, go to the doctor).

  Si vas a la playa, **ponte** *protección solar* (If you go to the beach, use suntan lotion).

  Echa *estas cartas en el buzón si sales* (Post these letters if you go out).

5. Fill out the sentences below with the appropriate word from the box.

> siempre – deja – cuando – encendemos – encontraré

1. Si nieva, *encendemos* la chimenea de leña.
2. Tomo helados _____ llega el verano.
3. _____ que aparcas ahí, te ponen una multa.
4. Si quieres tener buena salud, _____ de fumar.
5. _____ un buen empleo si termino la carrera.

6. Use *cuando* instead of *si* when possible.

1. Si no puedes venir, iré con mi hermana. _____
2. Si no puedo ir a mi clase, aviso a la profesora. _____
3. Si llueve en abril, la primavera es muy florida. _____
4. Si llueve en abril, tendremos que suspender el viaje. _____
5. Si te cansas de caminar, tomaremos un taxi. _____

7. Give advice, completing the sentences with the help of the prompts.

1. Si no quieres engordar, no/tomar/chocolate.
   ➡ *Si no quieres engordar, no tomes chocolate.*
2. Si quieres aprender inglés, ir/Inglaterra.

   _____

3. Si estás cansada, tomar/vacaciones.

   _____

4. Si bebes alcohol, no/conducir.

   _____

5. Si el bebé llora, cambiar/pañales.

   _____

8. Indicate if each sentence expresses a universal truth (UT), gives a piece of advice (A) or asks for a favour (F).

1. Si la temperatura baja de cero, el agua se congela. ➡ *UT*.
2. Si vas al supermercado, cómprame una barra de pan. ➡ _____
3. Si no quieres estar tan cansada, acuéstate antes. ➡ _____
4. Si ves a Teresa, dile que la estoy esperando. ➡ _____
5. Si estás cerca del Ecuador, el sol es más fuerte. ➡ _____

41   *NO COMAS LAS COMAS*
PUNCTUATION MARKS

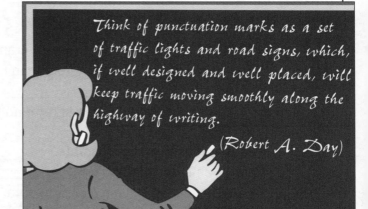

Think of punctuation marks as a set of traffic lights and road signs, which, if well designed and well placed, will keep traffic moving smoothly along the highway of writing.

(Robert A. Day)

- Punctuation marks in Spanish and English are basically the same, though they do not always follow the same rules.

- *Coma* (comma). It indicates a brief pause. It is used to separate elements in a list, to introduce explanations and to separate parts of a sentence. Also, when the name of the person addressed is introduced.

  Note that in Spanish no comma is used before **y** (and) or **o** (or).

  > *Me regalaron un chal, un bolso y unos zapatos* (I was given a shawl, a handbag, and a pair of shoes).

  > *París, la capital de Francia, es una ciudad grande* (Paris, the capital of France, is a big city).

  > *Tú estudias mucho, aunque tus notas no son buenas* (You study hard, although your marks are not good).

  > *Rosa, quiero hablar contigo* (Rose, I want to talk to you).

- As seen in unit 5, the comma is used in Spanish to indicate decimals. The full stop is used for thousands.

  > *El collar cuesta 1.235,85 euros* (The necklace costs 1,235.85 euros).

- *Punto y coma* (semicolon). It is a longer pause than a comma. It is used to separate the elements of a list which already contains commas, and also closely related sentences.

  > *Hay peras, uvas y manzanas en la nevera; patatas y tomates en una caja, y huevos en la cesta* (There are pears, grapes and apples in the fridge; potatoes and tomatoes in a box, and eggs in the basket).

1. Add commas and semicolons where necessary.

1. Me gusta tu hermano es trabajador educado y amable.

   ➠ **Me gusta tu hermano; es trabajador, educado y amable.**

2. El profesor hombre de mal genio entró en el aula.

3. Tomé ensalada pescado y helado de limón.

4. Ya sabes Luis que te aprecio mucho.

5. Vi a María más tarde hablando con su novio.

2. Decide if these numbers require a comma or a full stop.

1. Gana 2325 euros al mes. ➠ **2.325**

2. El café cuesta 125 euros. ➠ _____

3. Hay unos 25000 habitantes en esta ciudad. ➠ _____

4. Esa plancha de madera tiene un grosor de 0045 metros (45 mm). ➠ _____

5. Esta sala es muy grande; mide 235 metros de largo. ➠ _____

3. Correct the following sentences if necessary.

1. El mueble le costó 1,340.50 euros. ➠ **El mueble le costó 1.340,50 euros.**

2. Le gustan los chicos altos, rubios, atléticos, y de ojos azules.

   _____

3. Viajó en junio a Niza, Montecarlo y Cannes, en julio a Roma y Florencia, y en agosto a Praga y Budapest. _____

   _____

4. Le regalaron unos pendientes; un collar, una sortija, y una pulsera.

   _____

5. Mis padres viven en Madrid mi hermana en Segovia mis abuelos en Ourense, y mis tíos en Barcelona. _____

   _____

4. Add commas or semicolons where necessary in this text.

Mi abuela tenía siempre un regalo para cada miembro de la familia a mi madre le daba flores mermelada casera o fruta de su huerta para mi padre siempre tenía un buen puro para nosotras las dos niñas más pequeñas siempre había un juguete unas galletas caseras y un abrazo cariñoso.

41

NO COMAS LAS COMAS
PUNCTUATION MARKS

- ***Punto*** (full stop). There are three names for this punctuation mark in Spanish:
  - ***Punto y seguido:*** It separates independent sentences within the same paragraph.
  - ***Punto y aparte:*** It indicates the beginning of a new paragraph.
  - ***Punto final:*** It indicates the end of a text.

    Se acabaron las vacaciones. Ahora hay que estudiar (The holidays are over. Now we have to study).

- The full stop is also used necessarily at the end of an abbreviated word. For example, unlike in English, it is always used with abbreviated titles.

  El Dr. Rodríguez llegará pronto (Dr Rodríguez will soon be here).

- ***Dos puntos*** (colon). They are used to introduce a list or a quote, and in dialogues after speech verbs like *preguntar* (ask), *decir* (say), *contestar* (answer), etc. In Spanish correspondence, the colon is always used after the initial salute.

  Colecciona insectos: escarabajos, avispas y abejas (He collects insects: beetles, wasps and bees).
  El lobo preguntó: ¿Dónde vas, Caperucita? (The wolf asked: Where are you going, Little Red Riding Hood?)
  Querido Juan: ¿Cómo estás? (Dear John, how are you?)

- ***Signos de interrogación*** (question marks) and ***signos de exclamación*** (exclamation marks). There is only one difference between English and Spanish usage. In Spanish they go at the beginning and at the end of the question / exclamation (see unit 19).

  ¿Sabes quién ha llegado? (Do you know who has arrived?)
  ¡Qué cansada estoy! (How tired I am!)

- ***Comillas*** (quotation marks) are always double in Spanish. They are used at the beginning and end of a sentence for quotations, foreign words and the titles of books, films, etc., particularly in handwritten texts.

  "Ser o no ser, he ahí la cuestión", dijo Hamlet ('To be or not to be, that is the question', said Hamlet).
  Mi "hobby" es el fútbol (My hobby is football).
  Le gustó "Harry Potter" (He liked 'Harry Potter').

- The rest of the punctuation marks are used practically in the same way as in English.

5. Use exclamation and / or question marks where necessary.

1. Qué harías tú en su caso ➡ *¿Qué harías tú en su caso?*

2. Está equivocada o no _____

3. Si se entera tu suegra, pobre de ti _____

4. Qué película tan divertida _____

5. Si me hace falta (I need it) me ayudarás _____

6. Use quotation marks where necessary.

1. Acabo de leer Pepita Jiménez, de Juan Valera. ➡ *Acabo de leer "Pepita Jiménez", de J. V.*

2. Entonces pensé: No puedo esperar más. _____

3. Por lo general, nunca compro bestsellers. _____

4. Román dijo: ¡Qué historia tan rara! _____

5. Si quieres, vamos a ver Todo sobre mi madre, la película de Almodóvar. _____
_____

7. Use the appropriate punctuation marks.

1. Querida María nos vemos a las cuatro en el bar de la facultad.
_____

2. Mi madre siempre me dice lo mismo por qué no comes un poco más
_____

3. Escúchame hija por favor _____

4. Sevilla a treinta kilómetros y Huelva a sesenta son las ciudades más cercanas.
_____

5. Para el viaje utilizaremos el avión el autobús el tren te parece interesante
_____

8. Correct this text using the appropriate punctuation marks.

Ariel acababa de cumplir dieciséis años era la menor de todas las princesitas
marinas y también la más bella su piel tenía la suavidad de las perlas y sus ojos el
color del mar y al igual que sus hermanas no tenía pies su cuerpo terminaba en una
hermosa y brillante cola de pez Ariel era una sirena sin embargo a pesar de tener
todo el aspecto de una sirena no pensaba como una sirena porque ella estaba
enamorada de un príncipe que vivía en tierra firme como deseaba Ariel tener
piernas para poder marcharse con él quien podría ayudarla

42 AND, OR, BUT

LINKING WORDS

¡ YA ESTÁ BIEN DE PONERLE "PEROS" A TODO !

- Some words are used to link and relate words, parts of sentences or whole sentences.

  *¿Quién es: Pedro **o** Lucía?* (Who is it: Peter or Lucy?)

  *María lee **y** yo escucho la radio* (Mary reads and I listen to the radio).

  *Yo tengo mucho frío **pero** ella tiene calor* (I am very cold but she is hot).

- We use **y** (and) to link similar affirmative ideas. If the next word begins with **i** or **hi**, we use **e**.

  *La casa tiene dos pisos **y** el jardín es bastante grande* (The house has two floors and the garden is quite big).

  *Antonio es alto **e** Isabel es baja* (Antonio is tall and Isabel is short).

- As mentioned in unit 18, we use **ni** (neither) to link similar negative ideas. Sometimes **ni ... ni** are used (neither ... nor).

  *No quiero comer **ni** ver la tele* (I don't want to eat or watch TV).

  ***Ni** lo sé **ni** me importa* (I don't know or care).

  ***Ni** Felipe **ni** Eva hablan japonés* (Neither Philip nor Eve speak Japanese).

1. Use the appropriate form of 'and' *(y, e)*.

1. Tienen perros y / e gatos en casa. ➠ *Tienen perros y gatos en casa.*

2. Este negocio fue fundado por Román y / e hijos. _____

3. Mi hermana trabaja y / e estudia al mismo tiempo. _____

4. Me gustan las manzanas, las ciruelas y / e los higos. _____

5. Estoy cansada de escribir redacciones y / e historias. _____

2. Translate the following sentences into Spanish.

1. My mother has neither a car nor a bike.

➠ *Mi madre no tiene (ni) coche ni bicicleta.*

2. Neither my brother nor my sister want to come to the party.

_____

3. Please, tell me your name and your address.

_____

4. I don't like grapefruits or oranges.

_____

5. My parents and my grandparents were born here.

_____

3. Use *y, e* or *ni* as necessary.

1. Laura e / y / ni Pedro son mexicanos. ➠ *Laura y Pedro son mexicanos.*

2. Vete al comedor e / y / ni pon la mesa. _____

3. No lleva bañador e / y / ni sandalias. _____

4. Es muy terco e / y / ni independiente. _____

5. No entiende e / y / ni quiere entender. _____

4. Join the two sentences adding the adequate linking word.

1. Juan lava los platos *e* ⟍   a) es muy pesado.

2. Tengo hambre _____   b) quedarme en casa.

3. No quiero ir al colegio _____ ➤ c) Ignacio los seca.

4. Patricia tiene un perro _____   d) la nevera está vacía.

5. Tienes que trasladar el baúl _____   e) lo saca a pasear todos los días.

42

AND, OR, BUT
LINKING WORDS

- We can find words that link sentences expressing an alternative. Normally in Spanish we use *o* (or), again with the variation *u* if the next word begins with **o** or **ho**.

  Mis hermanos viajan en tren o toman el autobús (My brothers travel by train or they get the bus).

  Tienes que elegir entre clínicas pequeñas u hospitales en el centro de la ciudad (You have to choose between small clinics or hospitals in the centre of town).

- Some words like *pero* or *sino* (but) link opposite ideas.
  - *Pero* is used after an affirmative sentence.

    Estoy de acuerdo contigo pero lo haré a mi manera (I agree with you but I will do it my own way).

  - *Sino* is used to establish a contrast with a negative sentence. When followed by another complete sentence, *sino que* must be used.

    No fue Carlos, sino Elena (It wasn't Carlos, but Elena).

    No llegaron tarde, sino que fueron los primeros en llegar (They didn't arrive late; rather, they were the first to arrive).

- Both expressions can sometimes be preceded by a comma, to introduce a small pause which emphasizes the contrast.

  Julio trabaja mucho, pero su sueldo es muy bajo (Julio works very hard but his salary is very low).

- There are other words like *es decir* and *o sea* (that is to say) which explain the previous sentence. They always appear between commas.

  Ella es doctora, es decir, trabaja en un hospital (She is a doctor, that is to say, she works at a hospital).

  Se presentó de improviso, o sea, sin avisar previamente (He appeared suddenly, that is to say, with no previous notice).

5. Complete with *sino (que)* or *pero*.

1. Entré y no dormía, *sino que* estaba despierto.

2. Lo llamé por teléfono _____ no estaba en casa

3. No quiero hablar contigo, _____ con tu hermana.

4. Queríamos ir a la playa _____ llueve mucho.

5. No juegan al fútbol, _____ al baloncesto.

6. Correct the following sentences if necessary.

1. Todas las personas que quieran, mujeres o hombres, pueden solicitar el puesto.

➡ *Todas las personas que quieran, mujeres u hombres, pueden solicitar el puesto.*

2. Tienes razón sino prefiero intentarlo a mi manera.

_____

3. No perdimos el partido sino ganamos por dos goles.

_____

4. Es una chica muy guapa e usa una ropa muy elegante.

_____

5. Eres muy inteligente y suspendes las matemáticas.

_____

7. Translate these sentences into Spanish paying attention to the use of *o* or *u*.

1. Would you like apples or oranges? ➡ *¿Quieres manzanas o naranjas?*

2. You must throw away or organise these papers.

_____

3. Are you coming or are you staying here?

_____

4. I saw Oscar or Oliver, I can't remember

_____

5. I have biscuits or toast for breakfast.

_____

8. Use one of the following words to correctly complete the sentence:
y / o / pero / sino.

1. Estoy deprimido *pero* no sé qué me pasa (what the matter with me is).

2. Estoy triste _____ quiero llorar.

3. No estoy preocupado _____ muy contento.

4. Tienes que comer carne _____ pescado, lo que prefieras.

5. Debes dejar de comer pasteles _____ bombones para adelgazar.

43 I CAN AND I WILL
COMBINATIONS OF TWO VERBS

Querer es poder.

- In Spanish two verbs can go together; in this case the first verb informs us about the time and person who performs the action and the second one has a non personal form (infinitive, gerund or past participle).

> **Debes estudiar** *más el año que viene* (You must study more next year).
> **Sigue lloviendo** *muy fuerte* (It is still raining very hard; lit. It continues raining very hard).
> **Quedó aliviado** (He was relieved).

- Frequently the two verbs are linked by words like **a, de** or **que**.

> *Juan se puso* **a** *trabajar muy tarde* (Juan started working very late).
> *El correo acaba* **de** *llegar* (The mail has just arrived).
> *Los niños tienen* **que** *acostarse temprano* (Children have to go to bed early).

- The second position can be occupied by almost any verb. As for the first verb, it may indicate the attitude of the speaker. This attitude can be of obligation: *tener que* + infinitive and *deber* + infinitive. Note the difference with *deber de* + infinitive, which expresses a guess.

> **Tengo que** *trabajar esta noche* (I have to work tonight).
> **Debes** *vigilar tu dieta* (You must watch your diet).
> **Deben de** *ser las once* (It must be about eleven).
> *¿Quién llama?* **Debe de** *ser mi novio* (Who's calling? It must be my boyfriend).

1. Fill out the sentences with the correct word from the box.

deben – pone a – tienes que – deben de – acaba de

1. **Tienes que** ser más constante en tus estudios.
2. Ellos _____ irse a descansar.
3. Cuando se _____ comer, no para.
4. La película _____ estrenarse.
5. Son muy rubios, _____ ser extranjeros.

2. Put the verbs in brackets in the correct form.

1. Juan, (tener) **tienes** que estudiar más.
2. Mi padre (acabar) _____ de llegar.
3. (Seguir) _____ haciendo mucho frío.
4. No (deber) _____ ver tanto la televisión porque tengo dolor de cabeza.
5. (Tener) _____ que llevar a los niños a la playa.

3. Make sentences from these prompts with the verb in the first person singular.

1. tener que / limpiar la cocina ➠ **Tengo que limpiar la cocina.**
2. ponerse a / hacer los deberes _____
3. seguir / trabajar _____
4. deber / escribir una carta _____
5. acabar / salir _____

4. Translate the following sentences into Spanish.

1. You must visit your grandparents. ➠ **Tienes que / Debes visitar a tus abuelos.**
2. I don't have to go to school tomorrow.

   _____

3. My parents have to pay a mortgage.

   _____

4. This car must be washed.

   _____

5. You mustn't smoke in the bedroom.

   _____

43

I CAN AND I WILL
COMBINATIONS OF TWO VERBS

- There is an impersonal way to express obligation with *haber* + *que*.

    Hay que *limpiar esta habitación* (This room must be cleaned).

    No **hay que** *preocuparse* (You/One shouldn't worry).

- A way to classify the combinations of two verbs is to group them according to the feature of the action they refer to.

    – The first group tells us about the beginning of the action (see unit 36 for *ir a*):

    > *empezar a* + infinitive
    >
    > *comenzar a* + infinitive
    >
    > *romper a* + infinitive
    >
    > *estar a punto de* + infinitive
    >
    > *echarse a* + infinitive
    >
    > *ponerse a* + infinitive

    Empecé a *estudiar a las cuatro de la tarde* (I started studying at four p. m.).

    Estuvo a punto de *irse a Francia* (He almost went to France [but didn't]).

    Se echó a *llorar de repente* (He suddenly started crying).

    – Other verbs express the duration of the action (see unit 17 for *estar* + gerund):

    > *andar* + gerund
    >
    > *continuar* + gerund
    >
    > *llevar* + gerund
    >
    > *seguir* + gerund

    Lleva *lloviendo más de un mes* (It has been raining for over a month).

    Anda *saltando todo el día* (He is jumping up and down all day).

    Sigue *tosiendo mucho* (He's still coughing a lot).

    – Finally, there are verbs that inform us about the end of the action:

    > *acabar de* + infinitive
    >
    > *dejar de* + infinitive
    >
    > *terminar de* + infinitive

    Acabo de *decidir el menú* (I have just decided the menu).

    Dejó de *fumar por razones de salud* (He stopped smoking for health reasons).

    Terminamos de *recoger y nos fuimos* (We finished tidying up and we left).

5. Complete each of these sentences.

1. Mi padre acaba de *quitar la nieve del camino.*

2. Estoy a punto de _____

3. Tienes que dejar de _____

4. Mi hermana anda _____

5. El bebé rompió a _____

6. Choose the correct alternative in the sentences below.

1. El bebé *echó a* / ~~acabó de~~ andar de repente (suddenly).

2. Está a punto de / Hay que empezar a llover.

3. Vamos a / Dejamos de empezar un nuevo curso.

4. Acabamos de / Hay que llegar de viaje.

5. Lleva / Acaba haciendo mucho calor todo el verano.

7. Correct the following sentences if necessary.

1. El ciclista lleva pedalear todo el día. ➡ *El ciclista lleva pedaleando todo el día.*

2. Mi hermano acaba de terminando su carrera universitaria.

   _____

3. Sigue destrozar el castillo de arena.

   _____

4. La bomba estuvo a punto que explotando.

   _____

5. Su padre llegó de teniendo más de dos trabajos.

   _____

8. Choose the correct word.

1. El autobús acaba a / de llegar. ➡ *El autobús acaba de llegar.*

2. Tienes que / de comer mucha fruta. _____

3. Hay que / de arreglar esta bicicleta. _____

4. No dejes a / de practicar esta pieza de música; aún no la sabes.

   _____

5. Estuve a punto a / de llamarte para salir, pero me dio pereza.

   _____

44

HAVE YOU SEEN WHAT I HAVE SEEN?
COMPOUND VERBAL FORMS

- Apart from the simple tenses (past, present, future), formed with one single word, there are also several compound verbal forms. We will see two which refer to the past and one to the future.

¿ HAS VISTO LO QUE YO HE VISTO ?

- The first of these tenses is formed by the verb **haber** in the present + the past participle, and is used to express an action or a situation which started in the past and lasts until the present.

	-AR	-ER	-IR
Yo	**he** escuch**ado**	**he** perd**ido**	**he** viv**ido**
Tú	**has** escuch**ado**	**has** perd**ido**	**has** viv**ido**
Él/Ella	**ha** escuch**ado**	**ha** perd**ido**	**ha** viv**ido**
Nosotros/as	**hemos** escuch**ado**	**hemos** perd**ido**	**hemos** viv**ido**
Vosotros/as	**habéis** escuch**ado**	**habéis** perd**ido**	**habéis** viv**ido**
Ellos/Ellas	**han** escuch**ado**	**han** perd**ido**	**han** viv**ido**

- This tense is normally followed by a time expression such as *esta semana* (this week), *este año* (this year), etc., and also words like *aún, todavía* (same meaning: negative yet) or *ya* (already). Their position in the sentence is flexible and depends, as for other elements, on their length and relevance (see unit 2).

    ***He ido** de compras esta mañana* (I have been shopping this morning).

    *Los obreros **han trabajado** muy duro todo el año* (The workers have worked very hard the whole year).

    *Todavía no **ha llegado*** (He/She hasn't arrived yet).

    *Ya **ha parado** de llover* (It has already stopped raining).

1. Join each sentence in Spanish with its equivalent in English.

1. Ya he terminado mi desayuno. ➠ *c)*
2. La cocinera nueva ha preparado el menú esta mañana.
3. El autobús no ha llegado aún.
4. Los bancos han ganado mucho dinero este año.
5. Todavía no has arreglado el coche.

   a) The banks have made a lot of money this year.
   b) You haven't mended the car yet.
   c) I have already finished my breakfast.
   d) The new cook has prepared the menu this week.
   e) The bus hasn't arrived yet.

2. Write sentences with a compound verb using the prompts.

1. María / ir al cine / esta semana. ➠ **María ha ido al cine esta semana.**
2. Pedro / acabar las clases / este mes. _____
3. Los estudiantes / hacer muchos exámenes / este curso. _____

   _____
4. Antonio Banderas / rodar dos películas / este año. _____

   _____
5. Nosotros / escribir dos capítulos / hoy. _____

3. Use *aún/todavía* or *ya* to complete the sentences below.

1. **Aún / Todavía** no he acabado de comer.
2. _____ ha terminado la película.
3. ¿ _____ has visitado a tu hermana?
4. ¿ _____ no has leído el periódico?
5. Los niños _____ han llegado de la excursión.

4. Translate the following sentences into Spanish.

1. I haven't been to a museum for a long time.

   ➠ **No he ido a un museo desde hace mucho tiempo.**
2. We haven't seen the new film yet. _____
3. The teacher has just corrected the exams. _____
4. It has been snowing all winter. _____
5. I have made three chocolate cakes this morning. _____

   _____

- As seen in units 37 and 43, there are many words for expressing the recent past in Spanish, such as *desde* (since), *desde hace* (for), *hace* + time expression + *que,* and *llevar* + gerund.

    *Es hippy **desde** enero* (He/She has been a hippy since January).

    *Soy vegetariano **desde hace** un mes* (I have been a vegetarian for a month).

- *Hace* is impersonal and, therefore, invariable for person and number. *Llevar* changes according to person and number. Both verbs are very frequent.

    ***Hace** días que no te veo* (I haven't seen you for days).

    ***Llevo** toda la mañana haciendo ejercicios* (I've been doing exercises all morning).

- The second compound verbal form is also related to the past and it is formed by the verb *haber* in the past + the past participle of the main verb. It is used to indicate that an action or situation that occurred in the past and is now finished happened before another past action. The endings are as follows.

	-AR	-ER	-IR
Yo	**había** escuch**ado**	**había** perd**ido**	**había** viv**ido**
Tú	**habías** escuch**ado**	**habías** perd**ido**	**habías** viv**ido**
Él/Ella	**había** escuch**ado**	**había** perd**ido**	**había** viv**ido**
Nosotros/as	**habíamos** escuch**ado**	**habíamos** perd**ido**	**habíamos** viv**ido**
Vosotros/as	**habíais** escuch**ado**	**habíais** perd**ido**	**habíais** viv**ido**
Ellos/Ellas	**habían** escuch**ado**	**habían** perd**ido**	**habían** viv**ido**

    *Pedro **había terminado** la cena cuando María llegó* (Peter had finished his dinner when Mary arrived).

- The last compound verbal form connects the past and the future, because it expresses future but with a past projection. It is formed by the verb *haber* in the future + the past participle of the main verb. The endings are as follows.

	-AR	-ER	-IR
Yo	**habré** escuch**ado**	**habré** perd**ido**	**habré** viv**ido**
Tú	**habrás** escuch**ado**	**habrás** perd**ido**	**habrás** viv**ido**
Él/Ella	**habrá** escuch**ado**	**habrá** perd**ido**	**habrá** viv**ido**
Nosotros/as	**habremos** escuch**ado**	**habremos** perd**ido**	**habremos** viv**ido**
Vosotros/as	**habréis** escuch**ado**	**habréis** perd**ido**	**habréis** viv**ido**
Ellos/Ellas	**habrán** escuch**ado**	**habrán** perd**ido**	**habrán** viv**ido**

    *Cuando llegue junio, **habrán terminado** la casa* (When June arrives, they will have finished the house).

5. Complete the sentences below with a suitable form of *llevar* or *hacer*.

1. *Llevo* tres días sin dormir.

2. _____ mucho tiempo que no comemos juntos.

3. _____ un mes de retraso con el pedido.

4. _____ veinte años que no visitaba su pueblo.

5. _____ una eternidad sin bañaros en la playa.

6. Use the correct tense of the verb in brackets to complete the following sentences.

1. Cuando María llegó, la película ya *había acabado* (acabar).

2. Cuando María llegue, la película ya _____ (terminar).

3. Nosotros ya _____ (leer) ese libro.

4. La boda es en mayo; en octubre ya me _____ (casar).

5. Cuando Juan llegó, el tren _____ (salir).

7. Give the participle of these verbs. Be careful, they are irregular.

1. abrir ⟹ *abierto*   6. cubrir _____

2. escribir _____   7. hacer _____

3. morir _____   8. poner _____

4. romper _____   9. ver _____

5. volver _____   10. decir _____

8. Correct the verb *haber* in these sentences.

1. No habemos tocado nada.

   ⟹ **No hemos tocado nada.**

2. Este libro han tenido mucho éxito.

_____

3. Cuando el profesor llegó, los alumnos ya se han sentado.

_____

4. No sé quién te lo han dicho.

_____

5. Mi madre me preguntó quién me lo habías dicho.

_____

45 THE MOUSE WASN'T EATEN BY THE CAT
PASSIVE AND IMPERSONAL SENTENCES

¡EL GATO HA SIDO ZAMPADO POR EL RATÓN!

- Sentences can be active, when the subject is the agent of the action, or passive, when the subject of the sentence receives the action. This type of structure is used when the subject is unknown or unimportant, or to give prominence to another part of the sentence. In Spanish, passive sentences are far less frequent than in English.

  – Active: *Los alumnos **estudian** la lección* (The students study the lesson).
  – Passive: *La lección **es estudiada** por los alumnos* (The lesson is studied by the students).

- The passive verb is formed by the verb ***ser*** (to be) + the past participle of the main verb, which takes the same gender and number as the subject.

  *Los libros **son comprados** por el tutor* (The books are bought by the tutor).

  *Las jirafas **son fotografiadas** por los turistas* (The giraffes are photographed by the tourists).

- The subject of the active sentence may appear at the end of the passive introduced by the preposition ***por*** (by) or omitted altogether.

  *El helado es comido **por** la niña* (The ice cream is eaten by the girl).

  *El problema es solucionado **por** el técnico* (The problem is solved by the technician).

- In Spanish, only the direct object can be the subject of the passive.

  Una caja de bombones me fue dada /*Yo fui dada una caja de bombones (A box of chocolates was given to me / I was given a box of chocolates).

1. Decide if these sentences are active or passive.

1. La carta fue escrita por el rey. ➠ Passive.

2. La comida está preparada. _____

3. Los resultados serán presentados en la reunión. _____

4. Las tartas son decoradas por los pasteleros. _____

5. Esta playa estaba vigilada por la policía. _____

2. Choose the active or passive forms in the following sentences.

1. Cervantes *escribió* / ~~fue escrito~~ El Quijote.

2. *El Quijote* escribió / fue escrito en el siglo XVI.

3. Mi hermano fue contratado / contrató hace dos meses.

4. La factura ha sido pagada / pagó.

5. El nuevo centro cultural fue inaugurado / inauguró por el alcalde.

3. Match the two parts of the sentence.

1. Los precios de la fruta serán   a) dirigida por Almodóvar.

2. Cinco personas fueron   b) aumentados un 15%.

3. El viejo teatro será   c) desconectado para que no molestase.

4. La película fue   d) restaurado por un conocido arquitecto.

5. El teléfono fue   e) encontradas bajo los escombros.

4. Translate the following sentences into Spanish.

1. You will be sent the books.

   ➠ *Los libros te serán enviados. / Te enviarán los libros.*

2. The secretary was given the key.

   _____

3. They were offered a new flat.

   _____

4. He was asked some indiscreet questions.

   _____

5. I was sent a lovely bunch of flowers.

   _____

45

THE MOUSE WASN'T EATEN BY THE CAT
PASSIVE AND IMPERSONAL SENTENCES

- Another way to hide an irrelevant or unknown subject is via an active sentence with a third person plural verb and no explicit subject.

    Me dieron una caja de bombones (I was given a box of chocolates).

    Vendieron todos los cuadros de la exposición (All the paintings in the exhibition were sold).

- So far we have seen two uses of **se**, apart from the accented **sé** (I know; see unit 38). One of them is a personal pronoun for the indirect object (see unit 22). The other is a reflexive pronoun for the third person (see unit 34).

    Se *lo explicarán sus padres algún día* (His parents will explain it to him some day).

    Blancanieves **se** *miraba en el espejo* (Snow White looked at herself in the mirror).

- **Se** can also be used to indicate that the agent of the action is general and indeterminate (e.g., the general public). This impersonal use of **se** is often equivalent to a passive construction or to impersonal 'one' in English.

    En Vigo **se** *fabrican coches Citroën* (Citroën cars are made in Vigo).

    Se *dice que la enfermera por fin tiene novio* (It is said / People say that the nurse has a boyfriend at last).

    Se *habla inglés, francés y alemán* (English, French and German are spoken here).

    Cuando **se** *es joven, no* **se** *piensa en en la vejez* (When one is young, one does not think of old age).

- A more colloquial way to express the last sentence is with the verb in the second person singular form.

    Cuando **eres** *joven, no piensas en la vejez* (When you are young, you do not think of old age).

- Sometimes a **se** construction or a sentence with the verb in the third person plural form is preferred to the passive, if less emphasis on the subject is required, although the difference is subtle.

    La verja del parque **es cerrada** */La verja del parque* **se cierra** */* **Cierran** *la verja del parque a las doce* (The park gate is closed at twelve).

    Nada puede **ser hecho** */No* **se puede** *hacer nada /No* **pueden** *hacer nada* (Nothing can be done).

    Los ladrones **fueron detenidos** */ Se detuvo a los ladrones /* **Detuvieron** *a los ladrones* (The thieves were arrested).

5. Decide if these sentences are personal or impersonal.

1. En el norte nieva todos los años en enero. ➡ IMPERSONAL.

2. Hay muchos libros en el sótano. _____

3. Se lo diré a mi madre mañana. _____

4. Se condenó a los culpables. _____

5. Se lo terminarán todo en un minuto. _____

6. Translate the following sentences into Spanish using a *se* construction.

1. Smoking is forbidden in the library.

   ➡ *Se prohíbe fumar en la biblioteca.*

2. Fresh fish is sold here.

   _____

3. It is said that the king will come to Barcelona.

   _____

4. The new museum will be opened tomorrow.

   _____

5. Old and new stamps are bought and sold here.

   _____

7. Decide whether *se* requires an accent or not.

1. Se que me quieres mucho. ➡ *Sé que me quieres mucho.*

2. Se me olvidó tu número de teléfono. _____

3. Se cerró la puerta. _____

4. Se dónde está escondido el regalo. _____

5. Se pone furiosa cuando la insultan. _____

**8. Use the correct past participle to complete the passive sentences.
Be careful! The verbs are irregular.**

1. Este jersey fue *hecho* en China. (hacer)

2. El nuevo aparcamiento será _____ en abril. (abrir)

3. *El camino* fue _____ por Delibes. (escribir)

4. El problema fue _____ por la mejor alumna de clase. (resolver)

5. El cristal fue _____ por unos niños que jugaban al balón. (romper)

46 FOR OR AGAINST BULLFIGHTING?
WAYS OF EXPRESSING ARGUMENTS AND OPINIONS

- Argumentative texts present the advantages and disadvantages of something or the arguments for and against an issue. These reasons and opinions can be our own or other people's.

- These are some of the expressions that can be used to introduce the main aspects of the issue under discussion:

> *Alguna gente cree/piensa/opina que...* (Some people believe/think that...).
>
> *Una cuestión a tener en cuenta es...* (An aspect that must be taken into account is...).

- The very common Spanish verb *opinar* does not have a literal translation in English. It is usually translated by 'think', or by various turns of phrase like 'give/express an opinion', etc.

- If the opinion given is our own, we use specific expressions.
  > *En mi opinión* (In my opinion).
  >
  > *Creo /Pienso /Considero que...* (I believe/think/consider that...).
  >
  > *Por lo que a mí respecta* (As far as I am concerned).

- The arguments must be presented in an organised way, so we should use expressions to order them logically.

  > *En primer lugar* (First of all).
  > *En segundo lugar* (Secondly).
  > *Por último* (Finally).

  > *Además* (Furthermore).
  > *También* (Also).
  > *Tampoco* (Neither)

1. Match fragments from the two columns to form a sentence.

1. Creo
2. Por último,
3. Una cuestión a tener en cuenta
4. Algunos opinan
5. En primer lugar,

a) estos precios producen una bajada en las ventas.
b) debo señalar mi total apoyo a la propuesta.
c) que perderán el partido.
d) que esta reunión es muy importante para el futuro de la empresa.
e) es el precio del petróleo.

2. Fill in the blanks with the correct verb.

> continuar – terminar – comenzar

1. Para _____, podemos tomar unos aperitivos con un vino blanco.
2. Para _____, una carne asada acompañada con patatas y una ensalada.
3. Para _____, de postre tomaremos fresas con nata y un café.

3. Translate the following sentences into Spanish.

1. In her opinion English is a difficult language.
   ➠ *En su opinión el inglés es una lengua difícil.*
2. Some people believe that the conference was a success.
   _____
3. He considers that this sculpture is better than that one.
   _____
4. An aspect that must be taken into account is that it can rain.
   _____
5. My personal view is that you must finish the project.
   _____

4. Correct the following sentences if necessary.

1. En el segundo lugar, el trabajo es suyo. ➠ *En segundo lugar, el trabajo es suyo.*
2. Consideramos no es suficiente. _____
3. Algunas gente opinan que ha ganado el mejor. _____
4. Una cuestión a pensar en cuenta es el precio. _____
5. En mi opinión que, es la mejor solución. _____

- In order to express arguments in favour of an issue we can use the following expressions:

  Una ventaja es... (An advantage is...).

  Un aspecto positivo (A positive aspect).

  Estoy a favor de... (I am in favour of...).

- To express arguments against the issue we can use the following:

  Una desventaja es... (A disadvantage is...).

  Un aspecto negativo (A negative aspect).

  Estoy en contra de... (I am against...).

- Sometimes we need to introduce contrasting opinions. In these cases we can use:

  Sin embargo (However).

  Por el contrario (On the contrary).

  Por un lado... pero por otro... (On the one hand... on the other hand...).

  Por una parte... pero por otra... (On the one hand... on the other hand...).

- In order to rephrase or clarify an idea, the following expressions can be used (see unit 42 for others):

  Esto significa / quiere decir que... (This means that...).

  Lo que esto implica es que... (What this implies is that...).

- To give examples which support one or the other side of the issue, the most common Spanish expression is *por ejemplo* (for example), which is abbreviated as *por ej.* (e.g.).

  *Existen ciertos temas recurrentes, **por ej.**, el amor* (There are certain recurring topics, e.g., love).

- When we want to bring the discussion to an end, we can use several expressions:

  En conclusión (In conclusion).

  Para finalizar / acabar (To finish).

  Resumiendo (To sum up).

  En resumen (In summary).

  Para concluir (To conclude).

  Finalmente (Finally).

5. Read the text and fill in the blanks with the connectors below (use capital letters if necessary).

> resumiendo – en segundo lugar – por otro – mucha gente piensa
> por último – una última ventaja – en mi opinión – en primer lugar
> desde mi punto de vista – una desventaja
> otro aspecto positivo – por un lado

1. **Mucha gente piensa** que el mejor lugar para vivir es una ciudad grande.

2. _____, vivir en una ciudad pequeña es mucho mejor que vivir en una grande. Las ciudades pequeñas generalmente son más acogedoras y la gente tiene más tiempo libre.

3. _____, todo está más cerca y se pierde menos tiempo en desplazarse de un lado a otro.

4 _____, hay menos tráfico, por lo que también hay menos accidentes y muchos menos atascos.

5 _____ es que todo el mundo se conoce y, si te pasa algo, te ayudan; es como una gran familia.

6. _____ es que hay menos ruidos y se duerme mejor.

7. _____ es que las calles son a veces estrechas y se circula peor.

8. _____, hay menos posibilidades culturales, pocos cines, conciertos y teatros;

9. _____, no suele haber muchos museos y exposiciones interesantes.

10. _____, hay menos trabajo para la gente joven y menos tiendas donde comprar ropa de moda.

11. _____, a pesar de los inconvenientes yo prefiero vivir en una ciudad pequeña, ya que,

12. _____, tienes más calidad de vida.

47 THE WOMAN I LOVE

ADJECTIVE OR RELATIVE CLAUSES

- Some clauses or structures are used to modify nouns like an adjective does, so they can sometimes be substituted by one.

  *El chico **rubio** estudia inglés* (The blond boy studies English).

  *El chico **que es rubio** estudia inglés* (The boy who is blond studies English).

  *La muñeca **rusa** contiene muchas muñecas* (The Russian doll contains many dolls).

  *La muñeca, **que es rusa,** contiene muchas muñecas* (The doll, which is Russian, contains many dolls).

LA MUJER QUE YO AMO.

- Note that ***que*** is the most typical word used to introduce these clauses and it corresponds to all the English words: 'who', 'whom', 'which' and 'that'. Unlike in English, ***que*** can never be omitted.

- These modifying structures give further information about one of the entities in the sentence. If we give unimportant or even redundant information, the clause must appear between commas, but if we specify a feature that helps to distinguish the entity from others, it does not have commas, just like in English.

  *Mi hermana, **que tiene anginas,** no puede cantar* (My sister, who has tonsillitis, can't sing).

  *El coche **que me compré ayer** es muy rápido* (The car that I bought yesterday is very fast).

- ***Que*** can sometimes be preceded by a preposition (e.g., *a, de, en, para, por*) which slightly changes its meaning. The article that goes with the noun to which *que* refers may be repeated before *que*.

  *La persona **a la que** me refiero no está aquí* (The person whom I refer to is not here).

  *Las carreteras **por las que** vinimos ayer eran muy sinuosas* (The roads by which we came yesterday were very winding).

1. Substitute the modifier using *que* + an adequate clause.

1. La maquinaria de importación es muy potente.

➠ **La maquinaria, que es de importación, es muy potente.**

2. Ellos han instalado una piscina muy grande. _____

3. El niño vestido de payaso es mi sobrino. _____

4. La señora sentada en el sofá tiene un traje de alta costura. _____

5. Los alumnos hacen excursiones educativas. _____

2. Add commas to the sentences below if necessary.

1. Pedro que es dentista acaba de regresar de Francia.

➠ **Pedro, que es dentista, acaba de regresar de Francia.**

2. Sara compró una novela que está escrita en ruso.

3. El avión que acaba de aterrizar no llega con retraso.

4. Los árboles que están secos se cortarán mañana.

5. Las cajas tienen muchos lazos que son de colores vivos.

3. Correct the following sentences if necessary.

1. Tengo una maleta es gris. ➠ *Tengo una maleta gris. / Tengo una maleta que es gris.*

2. Juan que es enfermero trabaja en el hospital. _____

3. Las niñas tienen muchas madejas de lana, que son azules. _____

4. La caja, que tiene la marca, es para mi cuñada. _____

5. Ayer vendimos un barco qué tiene dos mástiles. _____

4. Join the two sentences into one using *que*, making the necessary changes.

1. Voy a salir esta tarde con una chica. Esa chica es inglesa.

➠ **Voy a salir esta tarde con una chica que es inglesa.**

2. Ayer te presenté a un compañero. Ese compañero se llama Javier.

_____

3. He leído *Historia de una escalera*. *Historia de una escalera* es una obra de Buero Vallejo. _____

4. Ya sé la marca del frigorífico. Voy a comprar ese frigorífico.

_____

5. Busco a una gatita desaparecida. Esa gatita es siamesa y toda blanca.

_____

THE WOMAN I LOVE
ADJECTIVE OR RELATIVE CLAUSES

- *Que* can be substituted by any of these words: ***el/la cual, los/las cuales,*** depending on the gender and number of the word they refer to. These words are less frequent and normally found in formal speech and written texts, after a preposition (e.g., *a la cual*, 'to whom') or sequence (e.g., *todos los cuales*, 'all of which').

    *La mesa, **que** está rota, es de roble /?La mesa, **la cual** está rota, es de roble* (The table, which is broken, is made of oak).

    *Se han reunido con las víctimas, **las cuales** consideran la indemnización insuficiente* (They have had a meeting with the victims, who consider the indemnification to be insufficient).

    *Se han examinado los aspirantes, **algunos de los cuales** han sido felicitados por el tribunal* (The candidates have been examined, some of which have been congratulated by the panel).

- Depending on the meaning, we can sometimes substitute some of these longer sequences (e.g., *en los que*) by ***donde*** ('where'), if they specify a location.

    *La casa **en la que** veraneaba está en Acapulco /La casa **donde** veraneaba está en Acapulco* (The house where I used to spend my summer holidays is in Acapulco).

    *Ése es el taller **donde** trabajo* (That is the workshop where I work).

- If there is a notion of possession, the introducing word is ***cuyo*** (and its related forms), which is equivalent to 'whose'.

    *La familia **cuya** hija es médico vive en el extranjero* (The family whose daughter is a doctor lives abroad).

    *Han llamado a las personas **cuyos** apellidos empiezan por P* (The people whose surnames begin with P have been called).

- When we refer to people, we can use ***quien*** ('who') and its plural, *quienes*, but, like in the case of *cual* and its related forms, it should only be done in very restricted situations, such as in formal and written contexts, and may be preceded by prepositions. Note the proximity between the noun and its complementing clause.

    *Lo decidirá la directora, **quien** toma este tipo de decisiones* (It will be decided by the head, who takes this type of decisions).

    *Lo dijo el primer ministro, **a quien** le preguntaron sobre el tema* (It was said by the Prime Minister, who was asked about the subject).

5. Make a single sentence out of each pair using the correct form of *cual*.

1. María trabaja en una fábrica. Yo también trabajo en esa fábrica.
   ➠ María trabaja **en la fábrica en la cual yo también trabajo.**

2. Los documentos están en el escritorio. El escritorio es de caoba.
   ➠ El escritorio _____

3. Han abierto un restaurante japonés. El restaurante ha recibido ya varios premios.
   ➠ Han abierto _____

4. Han nombrado un nuevo presidente. El presidente ha disuelto el parlamento.
   ➠ Han nombrado _____

5. El naufragio fue aquí. Una persona casi pereció en el naufragio.
   ➠ El naufragio _____

6. Add the correct preposition to the following sentences.

> a – para – en – por – de

1. El avión **en** el que viajan aterrizará en unos minutos.

2. La razón _____ la que llegamos tarde es que hay un gran atasco.

3. El examen _____ el que estudio es mañana.

4. La montaña _____ la que vamos está muy cerca.

5. La nevera _____ la que me hablaste es muy barata.

7. Fill out the sentences with the correct word.

1. El colegio **en el que / donde** estudiamos está en esta calle.

2. El chico _____ padre es actor acaba de llegar.

3. María, a _____ prestamos el descapotable, acaba de sacar el carné.

4. El parque _____ árboles talaron el otro día está muy feo ahora.

5. El cine _____ habían quedado está cerrado por reformas.

8. Translate the following sentences into Spanish.

1. The book which I am reading now is very exciting.
   ➠ **El libro que estoy leyendo ahora es muy emocionante.**

2. The village where we live is in the north of Spain. _____

3. I like the lady who is sat next to you. _____

4. My friend, whose parents are acrobats, will get married in the circus tomorrow.
   _____

5. Your sister-in-law, whom I saw yesterday, has lost a lot of weight.
   _____

WHERE WERE YOU DURING THE CRIME?
LOCATION AND TIME CLAUSES

- Some structures act as if they were adverbs: they modify or complement the main verb, providing different types of information (time, place, reason, etc.). Two of the most common structures of this kind are location and time clauses.

- Location clauses indicate the place where the action of the verb occurs. The most frequent word to introduce these clauses is **donde** (where). (See unit 47.)

    *Compré el libro **donde** me aconsejaste* (I bought the book where you advised me).

- When the verb or the sense of the sentence needs it, *donde* can appear preceded by a preposition. Note that the preposition **a** is joined to *donde* to form a single word. *Adonde* can be substituted by *donde*.

    *Pasearemos **por donde** no hace sol* (We'll walk where there is no sun).

    *Mis amigas irán **adonde** / **donde** les indiquen* (My friends will go where they are told).

- We must remember that *donde* can sometimes be substituted by *en (la/el/ las/los) que* (see unit 47).

    *Ésa es la oficina **donde** / **en la que** trabaja los sábados* (That is the office where she works on Saturdays).

1. Choose the appropriate preposition. Note that *en* is optional.

1. Han inaugurado el estadio *a / en* donde se celebrará el campeonato.

2. Pasearemos en / por donde están los niños jugando.

3. No miras en / hacia donde vas y a veces te caes.

4. Cruzaremos el río por / a donde cubre menos.

5. Los tigres se esconden a / en donde nadie los ve.

2. Join the two sentences with *donde* making any necessary changes.

1. Ése es el hoyo. Ahí tiene que entrar la bola.

➠ *Ése es el hoyo donde tiene que entrar la bola.*

2. Pon ese cuadro en la sala. En la sala hay otros cuadros.

_____

3. Mira hacia aquí. Yo estoy aquí.

_____

4. El gato estaba acostado allí. El sol daba allí.

_____

5. Me acerqué a la barandilla. La olas rompían en la barandilla.

_____

3. Correct the following sentences if necessary.

1. Éste es el lugar por donde nos conocimos. ➠ *Éste es el lugar donde nos conocimos.*

2. No me dijo hasta dónde iba a comer. _____

3. Saldremos ante donde nos digan. _____

4. Han derribado la casa para donde viví de pequeño. _____

5. Nunca sabemos de dónde ir de vacaciones. _____

4. Translate the following sentences into Spanish.

1. They go where their leader tells them. ➠ *Ellos van donde su líder les dice.*

2. The bicycle is not where I left it yesterday.

_____

3. You can take the bus from where I have shown you.

_____

4. We usually buy fruit where we can see that it has an organic label.

_____

5. My children study where I teach.

_____

WHERE WERE YOU DURING THE CRIME?
LOCATION AND TIME CLAUSES

- Time clauses show the moment when an action takes place. This action can be before, after or during another one.

- The most common time words are: **cuando** (when), **antes** (before), **mientras** (while), **después** (after), **tan pronto como** (as soon as), **en cuanto** (as soon as).

    *Fueron al polideportivo **cuando** terminaron sus clases* (They went to the sports centre when they finished their classes).

    ***En cuanto** llega la primavera, todo se llena de flores* (As soon as spring arrives, everything is covered with flowers).

    *Llamó **tan pronto como** llegó a París* (He called as soon as he arrived in Paris).

    *Leo el periódico **mientras** espero el autobús* (I read the newspaper while I wait for the bus).

    ***En cuanto** terminamos de comer recogemos la cocina* (As soon as we finish eating we tidy up the kitchen).

- When an action occurs before or after another one, the verb may be in the infinitve form.

    *Mándame un correo electrónico **antes de marcharte*** (Send me an e-mail before you leave).

    *Apagamos la television **después de terminar** el partido* (We switched off the television after the match finished).

- Another very common way of expressing that two actions occur almost simultaneously is the use of **al** + infinitive.

    ***Al acabar** de comer, fuimos de compras* (When we finished lunch, we went shopping).

    *Me di cuenta del error **al entregar** el examen* (I realised my mistake as I was handing in the exam).

    ***Al pagar** vio que no llevaba dinero* (As he was about to pay, he saw that he didn't have any money on him).

5. Fill in the following sentences with an appropriate time word or expression.

1. La reunión de la directiva se celebra *cuando* lo decide el presidente.
2. La cantante recibió muchos aplausos _____ terminó su actuación.
3. Escucho música _____ corrijo los exámenes.
4. Lorena se durmió _____ apagar la luz.
5. Le abrí la puerta _____ oír el timbre.

6. Change the structures in italics into an 'al + infinitive' construction.

1. *Cuando salí de casa,* me di cuenta de que no tenía las llaves.
   ➡ **Al salir de casa me di cuenta de que no tenía las llaves.**
2. *En cuanto llega al campamento,* me llama por teléfono.
   _____
3. *Tan pronto como recibí el ramo de flores,* leí la nota.
   _____
4. *Cuando acaba la película,* vamos a tomar un helado.
   _____
5. *En cuanto terminé la tabla de ejercicios,* fui a la sauna.
   _____

7. Join the pairs of sentences using different time words. Make any necessary changes to the second sentence.

1. No saliste con tus amigos. Ordenar tu habitación.
   ➡ **No saliste con tus amigos hasta que ordenaste tu habitación.**
2. Me llamó por teléfono. Llegar a casa. _____
3. Llegamos a la playa. Ponerse el sol. _____
4. Visité el museo del Prado. Ir a Madrid. _____
5. Fuimos a cenar. Terminar la película. _____

8. Translate the sentences below into Spanish, using a different time word in each case.

1. I wrote to him as soon as I heard the news. _____
2. She did the work before going out for a walk. _____
3. He fell asleep as soon as the film started. _____
4. I'll visit him while he is in hospital. _____
5. The children are playing basketball while their parents are having a chat. _____
   _____

49

WHY? BECAUSE

REASON CLAUSES

- A reason clause is used when we want to explain why somebody does something or why something happens.

- The typical words which introduce reason clauses are: **porque** (because), **como**, **pues**, **puesto que** and **ya que** (all of these are different translations of 'since' or 'as'). The reason can come before or after the main clause. The question 'why' is normally translated by **por qué**.

    Como no llegabas, me marché (As you didn't arrive, I left).

    ¿Por qué no responden? Porque no les interesa (Why don't they answer? Because they are not interested).

    Invitaré a Nicolás, puesto que es mi amigo (I'll invite Nicholas, as he is my friend).

- Other less common ways of introducing this type of structures are: **gracias a** (thanks to), **debido a** (due to), **en vista de** (due to the fact that), all of them followed by **que**. Another possibility is using the word **por** followed by the infinitive.

    *Lo ha logrado **gracias a que** su familia lo apoya* (He has achieved it thanks to his family's support).

    ***En vista de que** no os interesa, no os llevaremos al museo* (We won't take you to the museum due to the fact that you're not interested).

    *La niña se cayó **por** correr muy deprisa* (The girl fell down because she was running too fast).

    *No puedo comprar el coche **por** no tener dinero* (I can't buy the car as I don't have the money).

1. Fill out the sentences with the correct word from the box.

> como – porque – gracias a que – debido a – por

1. Aprobó los exámenes **por** estudiar todos los días.
2. No terminó la carrera _____ la muerte de su padre.
3. No vamos a la discoteca _____ estamos cansados.
4. _____ tienes frío, te presto esta chaqueta.
5. Llegamos a tiempo _____ nos llevaron en coche.

2. Match the two parts of the sentences.

1. Llévate un abrigo   a) ya que éste se estropeó.
2. Aprobó el test   b) porque hace mucho frío.
3. Te acompañaré al cine   c) pues hay corriente.
4. Cierra la puerta,   d) gracias a que le ayudé a prepararlo.
5. Compraremos otro motor, e) puesto que insistes.

3. Translate these sentences into Spanish.

1. Since it is Sunday, I will stay in bed all morning.
 ➡ *Como es domingo, me quedaré en la cama toda la mañana.*
2. I couldn't go to the wedding, because I was out of the country.

 _____

3. As the weather was good, we took the children to the beach.

 _____

4. I have given up sweets because I don't want to put on weight.

 _____

5. He sat all by himself because he was angry with his friends.

 _____

4. Finish the sentences with the prompts using *por* and an infinitive (affirmative or negative).

1. Perdió el tren **por no levantarse temprano** (get up early).
2. Se lastimó mucho _____ (wear a seat belt).
3. Llegué tarde a la cita _____ (wait for you).
4. Me quedaré hasta el viernes _____ (leave you alone).
5. La vaca está tan gorda _____ (eat too much).

49 WHY? BECAUSE
REASON CLAUSES

- Manner clauses indicate how the action takes place and usually come after the main clause. They are normally introduced by **como** and **según** (like or as). There is practically no difference between the two and most times they can be used interchangeably. **Tal como** is emphatic (just like/as).

  *Hemos hecho el trabajo **como/según** nos dijo el profesor* (We have done the work as the teacher told us).

  *Siguió la ruta **según/como** les indicaba el mapa* (He followed the route as the map indicated).

  *Lo hizo **tal como** se lo había pedido* (He/She did it just as I had asked him/her to)

- We will now make a few remarks about the spelling of some of the words used to introduce clauses: *porque* and *como*.

- Attention must be paid to **porque**, because there are three possibilities which must be clearly distinguished:
  - **por qué**, in two words, with an accent: it is the question 'why' (both in direct and indirect questions);
  - **porque**, in one word and without an accent: it is translated as 'because';
  - **porqué**, in one word but with an accent: it is a noun which means 'reason' or 'cause'. It can be singular or plural.

    *¿**Por qué** estás tan contenta? **Porque** acabo de aprobar el examen* (Why are you so happy? Because I have just passed the exam).

    *No conozco el **porqué** de su tristeza* (I don't know the reason for his/her sadness.)

- As seen so far, **como** has different values. It can show manner, reason or comparison. It only takes an accent when it appears in a direct or indirect question or an exclamation.

    *¡**Cómo** me alegro de verte!* (I'm so happy to see you!)

    *¿**Cómo** has llegado hasta aquí?* (How did you get here?)

    *No sé **cómo** lo hace* (I don't know how he does it).

    *Es tan lista **como** lo era su madre* (She is as clever as her mother was).

5. Translate these sentences using *como* or *según*.

1. You must write the composition as the teacher showed you.

➠ *Debes escribir la redacción como te mostró el profesor.*

2. The boys will follow the route as it is indicated in the plan.

_____

3. I want to plan my holidays as I like them.

_____

4. I will make the omelette as you like it, without onion.

_____

5. I don't like people who behave like he does.

_____

6. Complete with *porque, por qué* or *porqué*.

1. ¿**Por qué** no vienes conmigo?

2. No tengo _____ darte explicaciones.

3. La novela no me gustó _____ es demasiado complicada.

4. ¿Quién sabe el _____ de su reacción?

5. Mis amigos me quieren _____ siempre estoy dispuesto (ready) a ayudarles.

7. Complete the following sentences with *como* or *cómo*.

1. ¡**Cómo** siento tu ausencia!

2. Le pregunté _____ había salido la operación.

3. Si llueve, ¿_____ vamos a hacer el viaje?

4. _____ no me llamaste por teléfono, supuse que no querías venir.

5. Es tan guapa _____ su hermana.

8. Correct the following sentences if necessary.

1. Los alumnos preguntaron porque no les daban las notas.

➠ *Los alumnos preguntaron por qué no les daban las notas.*

2. Como te dijo la maquilladora tienes que pintarte.

_____

3. En esta vida todo tiene un por qué. _____

4. Actuaron bien segun las circunstancias. _____

5. Rosa preguntó como llegaron tan tarde. _____

50 QUERIDO ALUMNO
HAVING A TELEPHONE CONVERSATION
AND WRITING A LETTER

- Here are some tips for telephone conversations:

  – *¿Diga? ¿Dígame? ¿Hola? ¿Bueno?* (only in Latin America) (Hello?)

  – *¿Está María?* (Is that María?)

  – *¿De parte de quién? ¿Quién habla? ¿Quién la llama?* (Who's speaking?)

  – *Soy Juan. Quisiera hablar con María* (It's Juan. I would like to talk to María).

  – *No está en casa en este momento. ¿Quiere dejar un recado?* (She's not at home at the moment. Would you like to leave a message?)

  – *¿Podría/Puede decirle que me llame?* (Could/Can you ask her to ring me?)

  – *Claro, no se preocupe* (Of course, don't worry).

  – *Gracias, adiós* (Thank you, goodbye).

  – *¡Espere un momento, me parece que llega ahora!* (Hang on a minute, I think she's just arrived!)

Put these telephone conversations in the correct order.

1. a) En este momento no está. ¿Puede llamar más tarde?

   b) Por supuesto. ¿De parte de quién?

   c) ¿Podría hablar con la Sra. Luisa López?

   d) No me va a ser posible ¿Puedo dejarle un recado?

2. a) ¿De parte de quién?

   b) Hola, ¿está Susana?

   c) Espera un momento, ahora se pone.

   d) ¡Susana, te llaman por teléfono!

   e) Soy Cristóbal.

3. a) Gracias. Ya tengo su número.

   b) Ahora no está. ¿Quiere dejarle un recado?

   c) Querría hablar con el electricista, por favor.

   d) Puede llamarle al móvil.

   e) Es muy urgente. ¿Cómo puedo localizarlo?

4. a) Buenos días, ¿María Estévez, por favor?

   b) No, lo siento, en este momento no puedo atenderle.

   c) ¿Diga?

   d) Sí, soy yo, ¿quién es?

   e) Le llamo de una compañía de seguros, ¿tiene un momento?

   f) Muy bien, muchas gracias, Sra. Estévez, sobre las ocho hablamos.

   g) ¿Podría llamarla en otro momento?

   h) A usted, hasta luego.

   i) Esta tarde a última hora, sobre las ocho.

50

QUERIDO ALUMNO
HAVING A TELEPHONE CONVERSATION AND WRITING A LETTER

- Correspondence in Spanish is very similar to correspondence in English; there are two basic types of letters, formal and informal. The differences include punctuation and the opening and closing formulae.

- If the full address is not given, the date is written in the top right-hand corner, preceded by the sender's location: *Vigo, 19 de junio de 2005*.

- The sender's address is written on the back of the envelope; it is not usually included in the letter itself, especially in informal correspondence. To address the envelope, the use of *Don (D.)* or *Doña (Dña.)* is only possible if the first name is included (see unit 20).

  Don Luis Domínguez   Doña Engracia Martínez

- There is an increasing tendency towards simplicity in opening and closing formulae. For formal and business letters we can use: *estimado/a/os/as* or *muy señor/señora mío/a*.

  Estimado señor (followed by the surname, if known).

  Muy señor mío (with all the gender and number variations). This formula is not used with the surname and, therefore, is more common when the identity of the addressee is unknown to the writer.

- In private letters to friends or family it is very common to use *querido/a/os/as*. If the relationship is friendly but less close, *estimado/a/os/as* may be used.

  Querido Alberto   Querida tía Carmen   Queridos amigos
  Estimado Luis   Estimada Sra. Domínguez

- Note that in Spanish there is a clear difference in closeness between *querido* and *estimado*. In English both are translated by 'dear'. The degree of familiarity is also conveyed by the use of the first name or the surname, and by the use of *tú* or *usted*. All of the above formulae are followed by a colon (:).

- The most commonly used formulae for closing formal and business letters are:

  Un cordial saludo   Atentamente (le/les saluda)

- For private letters here are some examples of the many different combinations which (as in English) can be made.

  Un (fuerte) abrazo (Hugs)   *Tu hijo que te quiere* (Your loving son)

5. One of these letters is formal and the other one, informal. Complete them with appropriate opening and closing formulae.

1

_____ Mary y Pedro:

Me alegra mucho saber que habéis decidido casaros.

Os agradezco mucho la invitación. Por supuesto que estaré con vosotros el día de vuestra boda para desearos lo mejor.

_____

Luisa

2

_____ Sr. Pérez:

Le escribo para comunicarle que me interesa mucho la oferta de trabajo que me ha hecho su empresa.

Le agradecería que me indicase qué día y hora serían convenientes para mantener una entrevista.

_____

Luis González Armada

ANNEXE

1. IRREGULAR VERBS

2. GLOSSARY

Annexe 1. Irregular verbs

Verb	Present (Unit 10)	Gerund (Unit 17)	Commands (Unit 27)	
andar	ando andas anda andamos andáis andan	andando	anda ande andemos andad anden	
caber	**quepo** cabes cabe cabemos cabéis caben	cabiendo	cabe **quepa** **quepamos** cabed **quepan**	
cerrar (serrar)	**cierro** **cierras** **cierra** cerramos cerráis **cierran**	cerrando	**cierra** **cierre** cerremos cerrad **cierren**	
comenzar (empezar)	**comienzo** **comienzas** **comienza** comenzamos comenzáis **comienzan**	comenzando	**comienza** **comience** **comencemos** comenzad **comiencen**	
conducir (producir)	**conduzco** conduces conduce conducimos conducís conducen	conduciendo	conduce **conduzca** **conduzcamos** conducid **conduzcan**	
conocer (nacer)	**conozco** conoces conoce conocemos conocéis conocen	conociendo	conoce **conozca** **conozcamos** conoced **conozcan**	

IMPERFECT (UNIT 28)	PRETERIT (UNIT 28)	FUTURE (UNIT 36)	PAST PARTICIPLE (UNIT 44)
andaba	**anduve**	andaré	andado
andabas	**anduviste**	andarás	
andaba	**anduvo**	andará	
andábamos	**anduvimos**	andaremos	
andabais	**anduvisteis**	andaréis	
andaban	**anduvieron**	andarán	
cabía	**cupe**	**cabré**	cabido
cabías	**cupiste**	**cabrás**	
cabía	**cupo**	**cabrá**	
cabíamos	**cupimos**	**cabremos**	
cabíais	**cupisteis**	**cabréis**	
cabían	**cupieron**	**cabrán**	
cerraba	cerré	cerraré	cerrado
cerrabas	cerraste	cerrarás	
cerraba	cerró	cerrará	
cerrábamos	cerramos	cerraremos	
cerrabais	cerrasteis	cerraréis	
cerraban	cerraron	cerrarán	
comenzaba	**comencé**	comenzaré	comenzado
comenzabas	comenzaste	comenzarás	
comenzaba	comenzó	comenzará	
comenzábamos	comenzamos	comenzaremos	
comenzabais	comenzasteis	comenzaréis	
comenzaban	comenzaron	comenzarán	
conducía	**conduje**	conduciré	conducido
conducías	**condujiste**	conducirás	
conducía	**condujo**	conducirá	
conducíamos	**condujimos**	conduciremos	
conducíais	**condujisteis**	conduciréis	
conducían	**condujeron**	conducirán	
conocía	conocí	conoceré	conocido
conocías	conociste	conocerás	
conocía	conoció	conocerá	
conocíamos	conocimos	conoceremos	
conocíais	conocisteis	conoceréis	
conocían	conocieron	conocerán	

Annexe 1. Irregular verbs

Verb	Present (Unit 10)	Gerund (Unit 17)	Commands (Unit 27)	
contar (encontrar, costar)	**cuento** **cuentas** **cuenta** contamos contáis **cuentan**	contando	**cuenta** **cuente** contemos contad **cuenten**	
dar	**doy** das da damos dais dan	dando	da **dé** demos dad den	
decir (predecir, desdecir)	**digo** **dices** **dice** decimos decís **dicen**	**diciendo**	**di** **diga** **digamos** decid **digan**	
dormir	**duermo** **duermes** **duerme** dormimos dormís **duermen**	**durmiendo**	**duerme** **duerma** **durmamos** dormid **duerman**	
entender	**entiendo** **entiendes** **entiende** entendemos entendéis **entienden**	entendiendo	**entiende** **entienda** entendamos entended **entiendan**	
estar	**estoy** estás está estamos estáis están	estando	**está** **esté** estemos estad **estén**	

IMPERFECT (UNIT 28)	PRETERIT (UNIT 28)	FUTURE (UNIT 36)	PAST PARTICIPLE (UNIT 44)
contaba	conté	contaré	contado
contabas	contaste	contarás	
contaba	contó	contará	
contábamos	contamos	contaremos	
contabais	contasteis	contaréis	
contaban	contaron	contarán	
daba	**di**	daré	dado
dabas	**diste**	darás	
daba	**dio**	dará	
dábamos	**dimos**	daremos	
dabais	**disteis**	daréis	
daban	**dieron**	darán	
decía	**dije**	**diré**	**dicho**
decías	**dijiste**	**dirás**	
decía	**dijo**	**dirá**	
decíamos	**dijimos**	**diremos**	
decíais	**dijisteis**	**diréis**	
decían	**dijeron**	**dirán**	
dormía	dormí	dormiré	dormido
dormías	dormiste	dormirás	
dormía	**durmió**	dormirá	
dormíamos	dormimos	dormiremos	
dormíais	dormisteis	dormiréis	
dormían	**durmieron**	dormirán	
entendía	entendí	entenderé	entendido
entendías	entendiste	entenderás	
entendía	entendió	entenderá	
entendíamos	entendimos	entenderemos	
entendíais	entendisteis	entenderéis	
entendían	entendieron	entenderán	
estaba	**estuve**	estaré	estado
estabas	**estuviste**	estarás	
estaba	**estuvo**	estará	
estábamos	**estuvimos**	estaremos	
estabais	**estuvisteis**	estaréis	
estaban	**estuvieron**	estarán	

Annexe 1. Irregular verbs

Verb	Present (Unit 10)	Gerund (Unit 17)	Commands (Unit 27)	
haber	he has ha **hemos** habéis han	habiendo	ha haya hayamos habed hayan	
hacer	hago haces hace hacemos hacéis hacen	haciendo	haz haga hagamos haced hagan	
ir	voy vas va vamos vais van	yendo	ve vaya vayamos (vamos) id vayan	
jugar	juego juegas juega jugamos jugáis juegan	jugando	juega juegue juguemos jugad jueguen	
mentir	miento mientes miente mentimos mentís mienten	mintiendo	miente mienta mintamos mentid mientan	
mover (remover, promover, doler)	muevo mueves mueve movemos movéis mueven	moviendo	mueve mueva movamos moved muevan	

IMPERFECT (UNIT 28)	PRETERIT (UNIT 28)	FUTURE (UNIT 36)	PAST PARTICIPLE (UNIT 44)
había habías había habíamos habíais habían	hube hubiste hubo hubimos hubisteis hubieron	habré habrás habrá habremos habréis habrán	habido
hacía hacías hacía hacíamos hacíais hacían	hice hiciste hizo hicimos hicisteis hicieron	haré harás hará haremos haréis harán	hecho
iba ibas iba íbamos ibais iban	fui fuiste fue fuimos fuisteis fueron	iré irás irá iremos iréis irán	ido
jugaba jugabas jugaba jugábamos jugabais jugaban	jugué jugaste jugó jugamos jugasteis jugaron	jugaré jugarás jugará jugaremos jugaréis jugarán	jugado
mentía mentías mentía mentíamos mentíais mentían	mentí mentiste mintió mentimos mentisteis mintieron	mentiré mentirás mentirá mentiremos mentiréis mentirán	mentido
movía movías movía movíamos movíais movían	moví moviste movió movimos movisteis movieron	moveré moverás moverá moveremos moveréis moverán	movido

Annexe 1. Irregular verbs

Verb	Present (Unit 10)	Gerund (Unit 17)	Commands (Unit 27)	
negar (renegar, regar)	**niego** **niegas** **niega** negamos negáis **niegan**	negando	**niega** **niegue** **neguemos** negad **nieguen**	
oír	**oigo** **oyes** **oye** oímos oís **oyen**	**oyendo**	**oye** **oiga** **oigamos** oíd **oigan**	
oler (moler, soler)	**huelo** **hueles** **huele** olemos oléis **huelen**	oliendo	**huele** **huela** olamos oled **huelan**	
pedir (despedir, vestir)	**pido** **pides** **pide** pedimos pedís **piden**	**pidiendo**	**pide** **pida** **pidamos** pedid **pidan**	
pensar (sentar)	**pienso** **piensas** **piensa** pensamos pensáis **piensan**	pensando	**piensa** **piense** pensemos pensad **piensen**	
perder (defender)	**pierdo** **pierdes** **pierde** perdemos perdéis **pierden**	perdiendo	**pierde** **pierda** perdamos perded **pierdan**	

IMPERFECT (UNIT 28)	PRETERIT (UNIT 28)	FUTURE (UNIT 36)	PAST PARTICIPLE (UNIT 44)
negaba	**negué**	negaré	negado
negabas	negaste	negarás	
negaba	negó	negará	
negábamos	negamos	negaremos	
negabais	negasteis	negaréis	
negaban	negaron	negarán	
oía	oí	oiré	oído
oías	oíste	oirás	
oía	**oyó**	oirá	
oíamos	oímos	oiremos	
oíais	oísteis	oiréis	
oían	**oyeron**	oirán	
olía	olí	oleré	olido
olías	oliste	olerás	
olía	olió	olerá	
olíamos	olimos	oleremos	
olíais	olisteis	oleréis	
olían	olieron	olerán	
pedía	pedí	pediré	pedido
pedías	pediste	pedirás	
pedía	**pidió**	pedirá	
pedíamos	pedimos	pediremos	
pedíais	pedisteis	pediréis	
pedían	**pidieron**	pedirán	
pensaba	pensé	pensaré	pensado
pensabas	pensaste	pensarás	
pensaba	pensó	pensará	
pensábamos	pensamos	pensaremos	
pensabais	pensasteis	pensaréis	
pensaban	pensaron	pensarán	
perdía	perdí	perderé	perdido
perdías	perdiste	perderás	
perdía	perdió	perderá	
perdíamos	perdimos	perderemos	
perdíais	perdisteis	perderéis	
perdían	perdieron	perderán	

Annexe 1. Irregular verbs

Verb	Present (Unit 10)	Gerund (Unit 17)	Commands (Unit 27)	
poder	puedo puedes puede podemos podéis pueden	pudiendo	 puede pueda podamos poded puedan	
poner	pongo pones pone ponemos ponéis ponen	poniendo	 pon ponga pongamos poned pongan	
probar (aprobar, encontrar)	pruebo pruebas prueba probamos probáis prueban	probando	 prueba pruebe probemos probad prueben	
querer	quiero quieres quiere queremos queréis quieren	queriendo	 quiere quiera queramos quered quieran	
saber	sé sabes sabe sabemos sabéis saben	sabiendo	 sabe sepa sepamos sabed sepan	
salir	salgo sales sale salimos salís salen	saliendo	 sal salga salgamos salid salgan	

IMPERFECT (UNIT 28)	PRETERIT (UNIT 28)	FUTURE (UNIT 36)	PAST PARTICIPLE (UNIT 44)
podía	pude	podré	podido
podías	pudiste	podrás	
podía	pudo	podrá	
podíamos	pudimos	podremos	
podíais	pudisteis	podréis	
podían	pudieron	podrán	
ponía	puse	pondré	puesto
ponías	pusiste	pondrás	
ponía	puso	pondrá	
poníamos	pusimos	pondremos	
poníais	pusisteis	pondréis	
ponían	pusieron	pondrán	
probaba	probé	probaré	probado
probabas	probaste	probarás	
probaba	probó	probará	
probábamos	probamos	probaremos	
probabais	probasteis	probaréis	
probaban	probaron	probarán	
quería	quise	querré	querido
querías	quisiste	querrás	
quería	quiso	querrá	
queríamos	quisimos	querremos	
queríais	quisisteis	querréis	
querían	quisieron	querrán	
sabía	supe	sabré	sabido
sabías	supiste	sabrás	
sabía	supo	sabrá	
sabíamos	supimos	sabremos	
sabíais	supisteis	sabréis	
sabían	supieron	sabrán	
salía	salí	saldré	salido
salías	saliste	saldrás	
salía	salió	saldrá	
salíamos	salimos	saldremos	
salíais	salisteis	saldréis	
salían	salieron	saldrán	

Annexe 1. Irregular verbs

Verb	Present (Unit 10)	Gerund (Unit 17)	Commands (Unit 27)	
seguir (conseguir)	sigo sigues sigue seguimos seguís siguen	siguiendo	sigue siga sigamos seguid sigan	
sentar	siento sientas sienta sentamos sentáis sientan	sentando	sienta siente sentemos sentad sienten	
sentir	siento sientes siente sentimos sentís sienten	sintiendo	siente sienta sintamos sentid sientan	
ser	soy eres es somos sois son	siendo	sé sea seamos sed sean	
soñar (sonar)	sueño sueñas sueña soñamos soñáis sueñan	soñando	sueña sueñe soñemos soñad sueñen	
tener	tengo tienes tiene tenemos tenéis tienen	teniendo	ten tenga tengamos tened tengan	

IMPERFECT (UNIT 28)	PRETERIT (UNIT 28)	FUTURE (UNIT 36)	PAST PARTICIPLE (UNIT 44)
seguía seguías seguía seguíamos seguíais seguían	seguí seguiste **siguió** seguimos seguisteis **siguieron**	seguiré seguirás seguirá seguiremos seguiréis seguirán	seguido
sentaba sentabas sentaba sentábamos sentabais sentaban	senté sentaste sentó sentamos sentasteis sentaron	sentaré sentarás sentará sentaremos sentaréis sentarán	sentado
sentía sentías sentía sentíamos sentíais sentían	sentí sentiste **sintió** sentimos sentisteis **sintieron**	sentiré sentirás sentirá sentiremos sentiréis sentirán	sentido
era **eras** **era** **éramos** **erais** **eran**	**fui** **fuiste** **fue** **fuimos** **fuisteis** **fueron**	seré serás será seremos seréis serán	**sido**
soñaba soñabas soñaba soñábamos soñabais soñaban	soñé soñaste soñó soñamos soñasteis soñaron	soñaré soñarás soñará soñaremos soñaréis soñarán	soñado
tenía tenías tenía teníamos teníais tenían	**tuve** **tuviste** **tuvo** **tuvimos** **tuvisteis** **tuvieron**	**tendré** **tendrás** **tendrá** **tendremos** **tendréis** **tendrán**	tenido

ANNEXE 1. IRREGULAR VERBS

VERB	PRESENT (UNIT 10)	GERUND (UNIT 17)	COMMANDS (UNIT 27)	
traer	traigo traes trae traemos traéis traen	trayendo	trae traiga traigamos traed traigan	
valer	valgo vales vale valemos valéis valen	valiendo	vale valga valgamos valed valgan	
venir	vengo vienes viene venimos venís vienen	viniendo	ven venga vengamos venid vengan	
ver (prever)	veo ves ve vemos veis ven	viendo	ve vea veamos ved vean	
volver (envolver)	vuelvo vuelves vuelve volvemos volvéis vuelven	volviendo	vuelve vuelva volvamos volved vuelvan	

IMPERFECT (UNIT 28)	PRETERIT (UNIT 28)	FUTURE (UNIT 36)	PAST PARTICIPLE (UNIT 44)
traía	traje	traeré	traído
traías	trajiste	traerás	
traía	trajo	traerá	
traíamos	trajimos	traeremos	
traíais	trajisteis	traeréis	
traían	trajeron	traerán	
valía	valí	valdré	valido
valías	valiste	valdrás	
valía	valió	valdrá	
valíamos	valimos	valdremos	
valíais	valisteis	valdréis	
valían	valieron	valdrán	
venía	vine	vendré	venido
venías	viniste	vendrás	
venía	vino	vendrá	
veníamos	vinimos	vendremos	
veníais	vinisteis	vendréis	
venían	vinieron	vendrán	
veía	vi	veré	visto
veías	viste	verás	
veía	vio	verá	
veíamos	vimos	veremos	
veíais	visteis	veréis	
veían	vieron	verán	
volvía	volví	volveré	vuelto
volvías	volviste	volverás	
volvía	volvió	volverá	
volvíamos	volvimos	volveremos	
volvíais	volvisteis	volveréis	
volvían	volvieron	volverán	

ANNEXE 2. GLOSSARY

Here is a list of the linguistic terms used in this book together with simplified explanations intended to help the reader follow the principles of Spanish grammar.

- **Abstract noun.** A noun which refers to an entity that is not perceived with any of the five senses (e.g., *love, freedom*).

- **Active sentence.** A structure in which the subject is the protagonist or agent of the action and appears before the verb (e.g., *The cat ate the rat. We are Swiss*).

- **Addressee.** The person that the speaker or writer is communicating with.

- **Adjective.** A word class with full semantic content (see **determiner**) whose main role is to modify the meaning of a noun or pronoun, qualifying it or stating one of its properties (e.g., *The sky is **blue**. Pass me the **big** one*).

- **Adverb.** A word class whose main role is to modify a verb, an adjective or another adverb (e.g., *He walks **very slowly**. They are **awfully** nice*).

- **Adverbial clause.** A subordinate sentence which acts like an adverbial complement (e.g., *I saw her **as I was on my way home***).

- **Adverbial complement.** A word or group of words that add information about where, when, how, etc. the verbal action takes place (e.g., *She played **in the park***).

- **Article.** A determiner that precedes a noun to indicate its type of reference: definite, generic, etc. (e.g., ***A** cat is **a** feline animal. **The** cat ran away*).

- **Auxiliary verb.** A verb with very little or no meaning of its own which precedes another one with which it forms a unit (e.g., *I **have** been. He **is** chatting*).

- **Clause.** A structure which contains a verb. It may be simple, when it coincides with the sentence; complex, when it consists of two or more co-ordinated clauses, or compound, when it consists of a main clause and one or more subordinate clauses (e.g., *They stood up and left*).

- **Complement.** It is sometimes used to refer to any of the elements that are used to complete the verb phrase (e.g., *I gave **the present to my friend at his party***); it can also be used to refer to a word or phrase which completes the meaning of a noun, adjective or verb (e.g., *He is easy **to talk to***).

- **Conditional.** A structure which expresses a condition on which the event alluded in the main clause depends; it is also used to refer to the verb of the main clause (e.g., ***If I were a rich man**, I **would give** all my money to the poor*).

- **Conjugation.** In Spanish, one of the three verb classes which determines the endings that a verb takes in the different persons, tenses, etc.; conjugations are usually referred to by the infinitive ending: 1st or '-ar', 2nd or '-er' and 3rd or '-ir' (e.g., *amar, temer, partir*).

- **Conjunction.** A grammatical word used to join two clauses together; it can be **co-ordinate,** when it joins co-ordinated clauses (e.g., *He greeted us **and** left*), or **subordinate,** when it joins a subordinate clause to the main clause (e.g., *They came **when** we called them*).

- **Continuous / progressive verb.** A verbal aspect used to express prolonged or continuous activity as opposed to a momentary or habitual activity; it is formed by a form of 'to be' plus a verb ending in **-ing** (e.g., *They **were working** until 5.30*).

- **Co-ordinated word / structure.** Each of the words, phrases or clauses joined to others of identical status (e.g., ***You always study hard** and **pass your exams***).

- **Countable noun.** A noun which refers to an entity that can be counted using cardinal numbers (e.g., *a slice, a coin,* as opposed to *bread* or *money*).

- **Definite article.** A type of article which indicates that the noun refers to a specific entity known by both the speaker and the addressee (e.g., ***The** chair has broken*).

- **Demonstrative.** A determiner or pronoun that provides information about the location, literal or figurative, of an entity with respect to the speaker and/or the addressee (e.g., ***This** pencil doesn't work; I want **that** one*).

- **Determiner.** A word class with very little semantic content of its own, which accompanies the noun to provide additional referential information about it (e.g., ***This** picture is pretty. **Which** game do you want?*).

- **Direct object or complement.** The element which refers to the entity directly affected by the action of the verb (e.g., *The doctor cured **the patient***).

- **Gender.** A morpheme which mainly indicates the sex of the entity; however, in Spanish non-sexed entities also have a gender morpheme (e.g., *desk* ➡ ***pupitre*** [masc.], *table* ➡ ***mesa*** [fem.]).

- **Generic.** A type of reference made to a whole class or category of entities (e.g., ***Whales** are mammals*).

- **Gerund.** An impersonal verbal form that often acts as an adverbial clause of manner in Spanish (e.g., *He came **running***).

- **Grammatical word.** A word with little or no meaning used to provide a semantic nuance or to play a grammatical role (e.g., ***some** cabbages; **She** is fond **of** hiking*).

- **Imperative.** A verb or structure whose verb denotes a direct command or request (e.g., ***Be** quiet! **Sit** down, please*).

- **Indefinite article.** A type of article which indicates that the noun refers to an entity that is either unspecified or unknown by the addressee (e.g., *I've met **a** wonderful girl*).

- **Indefinite.** A determiner or pronoun that alludes to an entity or one of its aspects in a non-specific way (e.g., *There is **enough** food for **whoever** wants it*).

- **Indicative.** A verbal mood that denotes that the speaker/writer believes the statement to be true (see **subjunctive**) (e.g., *He swam*).

- **Indirect object or complement.** The element which refers to an entity indirectly affected by the action of the verb (e.g., *The customer gave the money **to the shop assistant***).

- **Indirect question.** A structure, other than the two standard interrogative structures (e.g., *Do you love me? Who do you love?*), used to elicit information (e.g., *I wonder **who you are**. Do you know **who the president is**?*).

- **Infinitive.** An impersonal verbal form used as a verbal complement; in Spanish it often acts like a noun (e.g., *I want **to sleep**. They hate **to bother** others*).

- **Interjection.** A word or expression typically used in exclamations to express the speaker's emotions (e.g., ***Goodness me,** what a beauty!*).

- **Irregular verb.** A verb that falls outside the standard conjugation patterns in one or more of its forms (e.g., *eat – ate – eaten*).

- **Main clause.** A complete or independent sentential structure. In a compound structure, it is the one with the most prominent semantic content upon which the other clauses depend (e.g., ***They stayed indoors** while the children played outside*).

- **Main verb.** A verbal form with full semantic content within a compound verb; it is also used to refer to the verb of a main clause (e.g., *We would have **warned** you. I **don't know** what you mean*).

- **Modifier.** The function of nouns, adjectives and adverbs when they provide semantic information about a given entity, property or action (e.g., *a **really beautiful stone** church*).

- **Mood.** A grammatical feature of verbs which expresses the degree or type of reality of a sentence, as perceived by the speaker/writer; three or four moods are usually distinguished: indicative, subjunctive, imperative and conditional.

- **Morpheme.** One or more letters added to the end of a word to provide grammatical information such as number, gender, tense, etc. (e.g., *jump**ed**; toy**s***).

- **Nominal clause.** A subordinate clause which can have the same functions as a noun (e.g., *He told us **what he believed** [cf. He gave us **his version**]*).

- **Noun.** A word class with full semantic content (see **pronoun**) whose main role is to refer to entities (e.g., *a **cat**, two **buses***).

- **Number.** A morpheme that indicates whether the entity is singular or plural (e.g., *two seats*).

- **Object personal pronoun.** A personal pronoun that functions as either the direct or indirect object of the sentence.

- **Particle.** A small word with no meaning of its own which acts like a grammatical marker; its presence is determined by another one, like a verb or an adjective (e.g., *to* in front of an infinitive).

- **Partitive.** A word or set of words used to express a part of a whole, particularly with non-countable nouns (e.g., *a loaf* of bread, *two pairs* of trousers).

- **Passive sentence.** A structure used to hide or relegate an unimportant or unknown subject and give prominence to the object by placing it in the preverbal position (e.g., *The thunder was heard in the whole province*).

- **Past participle.** An invariable verbal form used to form compound tenses together with an auxiliary verb; however, it is sometimes used like an adjective (e.g., *Hamlet was **written** by Shakespeare. Mary eats a **boiled** egg*).

- **Person.** One of the three grammatical categories that refer either to the speaker/writer or a group which includes him/her (1st person), the addressee or a group which includes him/her (2nd person), or neither of them (3rd person).

- **Personal pronoun.** A pronoun which distinguishes the grammatical person, number and/or gender of the entity it refers to (e.g., *we* [1st pl.], *you* [2nd]; *she* [3rd sing. fem.]).

- **Phrase.** A word or group of words which has a function in a larger structure (e.g., *The lovely singer thanked the audience*).

- **Possessive.** A determiner or pronoun that provides information about who the owner of a given entity is (e.g., *This is **my** car, not **yours***).

- **Predicate.** The part of a sentence that contains the information about the action or situation of the entity referred to in the subject, i.e., the part of the sentence which is not the subject (e.g., *The dancer's performance **was as beautiful as ever***).

- **Preposition.** A grammatical word used to link a modifying or complementing phrase to a meaningful word (a noun, verb, adjective, etc.) (e.g., *The boat goes **along** the river. The man **with** freckles is here*).

- **Present participle.** A verb ending in **-ing** which is used in combination with a form of 'to be' to form progressive verbs (e.g., *I was **reading***).

- **Pronoun.** A grammatical word used to substitute a noun or a noun phrase (e.g., ***We** greeted the little puppy and **it** waggled **its** tail*).

Annexe 2. Glossary

- **Proper noun.** A noun that alludes to a unique entity; it is always capitalised when written (e.g., *Mary is my sister*).
- **Reflexive pronoun.** A pronoun used to refer to an entity which coincides with that referred to by the subject (e.g., *They wash and groom **themselves***).
- **Related form.** In this grammar, any of the conjugated forms of a given verb or any of the gender and/or number variants of a noun, adjective, pronoun or determiner (e.g., *eat – **eats, ate, eaten***).
- **Relative or adjectival clause.** A subordinate clause which can act as a noun or pronoun modifier (e.g., *The boy **who had blond hair** smiled* [cf. *The **blond** boy smiled*]).
- **Semantic.** Related to meaning; meaningful.
- **Sentence.** A complete and meaningful structure typically formed by a subject and a predicate, although one of them may be elliptic or omitted (e.g., *This is an example of a sentence. Read this!*).
- **Subject personal pronoun.** A personal pronoun that functions as the subject of the sentence (e.g., ***They** are the champions*).
- **Subject.** The person or thing that the sentence is about; the protagonist, the agent or the doer of the action (e.g., ***The cows** eat in the fields*).
- **Subjunctive.** A verbal mood that denotes the status of remoteness, unreality and possibility of the action as believed by the speaker/writer (cf. **indicative**) (e.g., *If I **were** you, I'd phone first*).
- **Subordinate clause.** A dependent or embedded sentential structure which provides further information (of time, location, manner, etc.) about some part or the whole of the main clause (e.g., *This is the city **where I was born***).
- **Syllable.** A letter or group of letters pronounced at the same time (e.g., *ma-chine*).
- **Tense.** A grammatical feature of verbs which locates the time when the event or situation described occurs (e.g., past, future).
- **Variable word.** A word which changes its form according to grammatical criteria such as tense, person, gender or number (e.g., *cat – cats*).
- **Verb.** A word class with full semantic content (except in the case of the auxiliaries) whose main role is to refer to an action, event, state or situation undergone by the subject (e.g., *went; had laughed*).

INDEX

Index